When We Almost Lost Israel

A Sailor's Tale of the Yom Kippur War

Albert Schriber

Dedication

To all those who served and participated in the 1973 Yom Kippur War:

This book is dedicated to the brave souls who fought on the front lines and those who helped from afar through the unstable days of the Yom Kippur War. Your bravery and commitment to duty created an unforgettable impact on history.

A particular mention goes to my shipmates from the USS John F. Kennedy. We weathered uncertainty and danger together, representing real friendship and sacrifice. Your unshakable commitment and support at those vital moments represent the finest of what it means to serve.

May your stories of bravery and dedication continue to inspire future generations.

With my utmost respect and gratitude,

Albert Schriber

Acknowledgment

I would like to express my deepest gratitude to all those who contributed to the creation of this book:

My fellow sailors on the USS John F. Kennedy, your company and support during our time at sea were essential. You made significant contributions to this story that are difficult to put into words.

I'm grateful to my family and friends for their tolerance and encouragement during this journey; your trust in me gave me the courage to share my stories.

To the historians, scholars, and military men who aided with the verification of the facts and gave new perspectives, your efforts were critical to guarantee the accuracy and depth of this work.

And to the men and women who fought alongside me in the war, your heroism will not be forgotten.

With sincere appreciation,

Albert Schriber

About the Author

Albert Schriber was born in the Touro Infirmary in New Orleans, Louisiana. His life is characterized by commitment, service, and technical skill. He spent twelve years in the United States Navy, establishing tremendous discipline and devotion.

Albert established a successful career in the technology industry following his military service. He worked as a computer engineer at Hewlett-Packard for 27 years, contributing to several breakthroughs and discoveries. His knowledge and zeal for technology have left an ineradicable mark on the business.

Albert's experiences, from his early years in New Orleans to his time in the Navy and at Hewlett-Packard, formed his distinct viewpoint and storytelling ability. His work displays a wide range of experiences, technical knowledge, and an awareness of the human spirit.

Albert, although retired, still likes writing and sharing his thoughts and tales with readers. He resides in Peachtree City, Georgia, and is an active community member who likes spending time with his family and volunteering.

Contents

Chapter 1: A Scottish Sojourn

"Never think that war, no matter how necessary, nor how justified, is not a crime."

- Ernest Hemingway, 1946

It was October 10, 1973, and tensions were running high in the Middle East. I was a sailor in the U.S. Navy returning after completing a mission on the Kennedy, the only ship of its class. She docked in Edinburgh, Scotland, marking the end of my five-month cruise. My shipmates and I eagerly looked forward to returning to the United States after being away for so long. We had just finished an exercise in the North Atlantic before arriving in Edinburgh.

Walking through Edinburgh's busy streets felt like everything was bursting with life. Old buildings and rich history pictured a different world from the endless ocean we knew. It was like time stopped just for us, letting us soak it all in before saying goodbye. My shipmates talked just like me. They were excited to get back and hug family again.

My friend and shipmate, Steve, and I decided to explore the town. There, we stumbled upon something unexpected- a Walgreens store, where we grabbed a bite to eat. Little did we know then that another assignment was coming our way. To wash over the exhaustion from a long journey, we decided to go to a pub and grab a few beers toward the day's end. We were drinking and having beer when two women entered the bar. They introduced themselves as hitchhikers. As we struck up a conversation with them, we found out about the outbreak of War in Israel. As we learned about it, a sense of unease settled over us. It was deeply concerning to us as our stay could be extended. And so, what we never expected came crushing our plans.

We received orders to mobilize, and I could not help but feel a mix of fear and anticipation. The U.S. had started an operation to protect our airspace and assist Israel in the Yom Kippur War. So, instead of heading back home, we found ourselves participating in several operations related to the Yom Kippur War. We streamed to a holding position 100 miles west of Gibraltar to provide support for Israel's top priority requests: forty-six aircraft, two hundred AIM-9 Sidewinder missiles, and anti-tank missiles and launchers. It was quite a twist of fate, I must say. However, it led me to witness the war closely and come up with insights into how it shaped history. This book is my narrative based on what I witnessed during the Yom Kippur War and how it is influencing the contemporary world.

Finally, after a brief sojourn in Edinburgh, we sailed to a holding position 100 miles west of Gibraltar, rejoining the Sixth Fleet and sticking around for a while. It was a tense and uncertain time, and I could not believe it when I heard the news for the first time. However, I only hoped for a peaceful resolution to this devastating conflict.

As the war raged, tensions increased with the silent clash between superpowers. October 6 is considered the holiest day in Judaism, Yom Kippur. On this day in 1973, Egyptian and Syrian forces launched a surprise attack on Israel, igniting what would soon be known as the Yom Kippur War. The attack aimed to regain control of the Sinai Peninsula and the Golan Heights, territories lost in the previous Six-Day War. As the war raged on, tensions rose in the Middle East, and many feared it would escalate into a full-blown regional conflict.

Suddenly, pressure was on President Nixon to provide more support for our ally. He tasked his Secretary of State, Henry Kissinger, to engage in shuttle diplomacy in an attempt to find a peaceful resolution. They were traveling back and forth between the warring nations in an attempt to broker a ceasefire. I knew our presence on the seas would play an important role in their delicate negotiations. But I also knew it meant that we would potentially be in harm's way.

Meanwhile, back in Washington, D.C., President Nixon faced intense pressure from his advisors to intervene directly in the war. But he was hesitant, not wanting to escalate the situation and potentially spark a larger conflict with the Soviet Union. It was a delicate balance, and the weight of the world seemed to be on his shoulders.

I could not help but wonder about the impact this war would have on the region and on our country's foreign policy. Nixon's détente policy during the Cold War was being put to the test, so I felt the weight of responsibility on our shoulders. During our time at sea, I witnessed firsthand the desperation of war. We provided support to cargo planes supplying Israel with much-needed weapons and equipment, all while trying to stay safe amid potential enemy attacks.

I was a young sailor fresh out of training and ready to take on any challenge that came my way. Little did I know the next few weeks would put my training to the ultimate test. We advanced 100 miles to the west of Gibraltar to fulfill Israel's most urgent demands. However, it was not until October 25th that John F. Kennedy received orders to rejoin the 6th fleet in the Eastern Mediterranean. She was responsible for protecting the air space in support of cargo planes by flying 150 to 200 sorties per day. Shortly after this, we received news that the U.S. Department of State had approved the transfer of F-4 Phantom and A-4 Skyhawk aircraft, along with other weapons to the Middle East.

Our country was indirectly embroiled in a conflict, and tensions were high. As we neared our destination, I felt a mix of excitement and apprehension. The world was watching, and all eyes were on the United States to see how we would handle the situation. Some, like President Nixon, saw this as an opportunity to showcase our strength, while others, like former President Kennedy, believed in a more cautious approach.

The U.S. government also announced Operation Nickel Grass, a critical lifeline for our ally Israel, who was facing heavy losses in the ongoing conflict. But despite this help, Israel refused to cease fighting, even after a United Nations ceasefire was put in place. They were determined to improve their positions and complete their encirclements, which only escalated the situation. The Soviets, allied with the Arab nations, threatened to intervene, and tensions rose to a dangerous level. Our ship was put on high alert as we were ready to take action at a moment's notice.

Then came the most alarming order: The nuclear high alert.

The threat of nuclear war was no longer just a distant possibility. Our mission was now not only to protect Israel and maintain peace in the region but also to be prepared for a potential nuclear conflict. It was a terrifying thought, but we were trained to handle the worst. As we sailed toward the Eastern Mediterranean to rejoin the Sixth Fleet, the tension on the ship was palpable. Our admiral's objective was to have our aircraft and weapons ready to launch within fifteen minutes of notice. It was a race against time, but we were determined to fulfill our duty.

While the military of both parties was in a direct confrontation, the great leaders of that time were lobbying to strengthen diplomatic ties. Gamal Abdel Nasser, a former Egyptian President, passed away in September 1970. Right after his funeral, Sadat wasted no time trying to win over Nixon and show him that Egypt was eager for some American love. Sadat's connection to the president was through the Secretary of Health, Education, and Welfare. Elliot Richardson, who at the time was Secretary for the Department of Health, Education, and Welfare, led the U.S. delegation to Nasser's funeral. During the funeral procession, Sadat had a little heat stroke scare and had to take a break. While everyone else waited in a tent, Sadat had Richardson taken to a nearby building's basement, where he was resting. Sadat warmly invited Richardson to a meeting the next day, where he asked him to tell Nixon that Egypt wanted to start fresh and have a friendly relationship with the United States.

Sadat kept up the charm offensive, and it paid off. In May 1971, Secretary of State William Rogers visited Cairo, the first one to do so since John Foster Dulles twenty years earlier. Sadat wasted no time and got straight to the point, telling Rogers that he wanted to get closer to the West and move away from the Soviet Union. He made it clear that the Arabs preferred the West and appreciated their values and business opportunities. Sadat even threw in a compliment about American businessmen just to sweeten the deal.

It was a clever tactic, knowing that the U.S. was a powerful ally of Israel. He was playing on our alliance with Israel to gain an advantage in the war. I was struck by the power of diplomacy during this crisis. As Nixon and Kissinger worked tirelessly toward a resolution, Sadat's ploy pushed for negotiations that would ultimately benefit Egypt.

As reports of Israeli losses began to pour in, the pressure on Nixon continued to mount. In response, we provided 200 AIM-9 Sidewinder air-to-air missiles and SHRIKE anti-SAM radar missiles. As the situation intensified, we also supplied tube-launched, optically tracked, wire-guided missiles and launchers, as well as light anti-tank weapons. These weapons gave the Israeli army the ability to fire 66 mm unguided single-shot anti-tank projectiles, significantly enhancing their defense capabilities. We soon learned that Israeli losses were even greater than initially thought, with 48 of their Skyhawk aircraft destroyed in the first days of the war.

As the conflict raged on, Nixon's foreign policy came under scrutiny. Some compared his approach to that of his predecessor, Ronald Reagan, who famously believed in "peace through strength." Others saw parallels with Theodore Roosevelt's mantra of "walk softly but carry a big stick." The discussions were ongoing, but little did we know what the future had in store.

But things quickly escalated. Our actions were in direct violation of a UN ceasefire, and the Soviet Union, who had been supporting Egypt and Syria, threatened to intervene. This is important as many reports and articles state that the Soviets didn't threaten to intervene, but they did! My heart raced as I listened to orders being shouted and the ship being put on Nuclear High Alert. It was a terrifying thought to be involved in a potential nuclear conflict.

As tensions reached a breaking point, we armed and prepared our planes, ready to launch at a moment's notice. Every sailor on board was on edge, knowing that the world's fate may rest on our actions.

Just when it seemed like all hope was lost, a breakthrough was made. Through the tireless efforts of our top diplomats, a ceasefire was finally negotiated, and the Yom Kippur War came to an end. Our hearts were filled with relief, knowing that our actions had helped bring peace to the region.

Looking back on those days, I am proud to have been a part of the Kennedy and its role in the conflict. We may have been just a small piece of the puzzle, but we never lost sight of our goal— to protect our country and its allies, no matter what challenges came our way.

However, in the aftermath of the war, I feel conflicted about the response and involvement of the U.S. in the war. Some criticized us for not intervening more aggressively, while others argued that we had done all we could without risking a potential nuclear war with the Soviet Union. It was a tough position to be in, and I found myself questioning our decisions every day.

As the conflict between the Middle East and the U.S. continued to deepen, I know that the lessons learned from the

1973 Yom Kippur War would forever shape our diplomatic decisions and actions in the region.

Reminiscing those days, I think about the fragility of global politics and the importance of strong alliances and diplomacy. The Yom Kippur War was a stark reminder of how quickly things can escalate and how important it is to work toward peace instead of conflict. As a sailor on the Kennedy, I was proud to have played a small part in helping our ally and preventing a larger catastrophe.

Although Israel had emerged victorious, the impact of this war would be felt for years to come. It continued to shape the relationships between the U.S., Israel, and the Soviet Union. And today, when the world is brewing with another war, the decisions made during that war have a remarkable influence.

On October 7, 2023, fifty years and one day after the Yom Kippur War began on October 6, 1973, I found myself pondering many questions from the past. It's crazy to think that if the United States hadn't helped Israel during that War, Israel might not even exist today. My shipmates and I aboard the USS John F. Kennedy were unexpectedly thrust into the conflict instead of heading home as planned.

I couldn't help but wonder: What if the United States hadn't come to Israel's aid? What if our powerful Navy had directly intervened? What if Israel and the Soviet Union hadn't agreed to the ceasefire? And why did the United States go to DEFCON 3?

But the question that really keeps me up at night is this: Could the wars we see today have been prevented back in 1973? It's a lot to think about, that's for sure. Although it occurred almost 50 years ago, its lessons continue to shape how we understand and approach this ongoing conflict. The war led to the emergence of non-state actors like Hamas during the Yom Kippur War. It has had a lasting impact on the conflict. The tactics they employed in their fight against the Israeli military are still being utilized today, demonstrating the influential role they have played in shaping the ongoing conflict.

My experience of the Yom Kippur War was a turning point in the history of Israel and its relationship with its neighbors. This war has had a profound impact on the ongoing conflict between Israel and Hamas today, shaping its dynamics in various ways. In 1973, I saw Israel, a tiny nation surrounded by Arab countries, face a surprise attack by its neighbors on the holiest day of the Jewish calendar.

Witnessing Israel's vulnerabilities and significant casualties, I came to understand the weaknesses of its military strategy. After this confrontation, Israel was forced to reassess its approach, shifting its focus to intelligence gathering and air power. This approach can be seen in their response to the current Israel-Hamas conflict.

As a result, I also became aware of the important role of external actors in influencing the conflict. I saw firsthand how countries like the United States and the Soviet Union played an important role and how this trend has continued in the ongoing Israel-Hamas conflict. I have seen the involvement of countries like the United States, Egypt, and Qatar in negotiating ceasefires and providing aid to the warring parties.

The Yom Kippur War also changed the way I perceived Israel. The previously perceived invincibility of the nation was shattered, and I witnessed the strength and resilience shown by its Arab neighbors. This has influenced the way I view the current conflict and raised questions about Israel's military actions and policies toward Palestinians.

Although the war militarily strengthened Israel, it also brought a peaceful end through diplomatic efforts and peace negotiations. Had Nixon and Kissinger not negotiated at the time of the Yom Kippur War, the world would have met with serious consequences. I have seen the need for a negotiated settlement and how the Camp David Accords 1978 resulted in a peace treaty between Israel and Egypt. Similarly, I have witnessed multiple attempts at ceasefire and peace negotiations in the current conflict, with the latest effort being the 2021 ceasefire mediated by Egypt.

As I witness the increasing intensity of the current conflict, I reflect on the lessons learned from the Yom Kippur War. It is a powerful reminder that violence is not always the solution and that peaceful solutions through negotiation and diplomacy can yield lasting results. The choices made during that war have significantly impacted the ongoing conflict and will continue to do so for the foreseeable future.

As the saying goes, *"Those who cannot learn from history are doomed to repeat it."*

This rings true in the current situation, as we must strive to find a peaceful solution that will bring about long-term peace and stability in the world.

"The mission of the Navy is to maintain, train, and equip combat-ready Naval forces capable of winning wars, deterring aggression, and maintaining freedom of the seas."

Chapter 2: Echoes of 1967

"To witness history is more often a curse than a blessing."

- Haruki Murakami

The summer of 1967 was unlike any other in my youth days, not just because of the adventures that typically filled the days of a boy my age but because of the war that erupted far away from my American hometown. As a teenager, the Six-Day War was a complicated concept for me to fully grasp, yet it seeped into my consciousness through the snippets of news broadcasts and the solemn conversations of adults.

From this distance, the conflict appeared as a sequence of noises and visuals, such as the radio's static, our television's jerky black-and-white pictures, and creases on my parents' heads. These were the first times I had ever encountered the reality of conflict, which felt incredibly intimate even though it lived in a world very different from mine.

Growing up in America, my view of the conflict was initially shaped by the stories I heard and the images I saw. These early impressions were stark, filled with the simplicity of good versus evil narratives often found in children's stories. However, as I aged, I began to see the shades of gray in the world.

It all began in the early days of June. The atmosphere was charged with anticipation and dread. The borders had become increasingly volatile, especially with the movements of Egyptian troops into the Sinai Peninsula and the expulsion of the UN peacekeeping forces by Egypt's President Nasser. Fears of an impending attack were stoked by Nasser's closure of the Straits of Tiran to Israeli shipping, which was like lighting a match.

I was just a young person then, but I could sense the gravity of the situation. Our leaders spoke of the need to defend our nation and take pre-emptive action to secure our future. And so, Israel launched a surprise aerial offensive that decimated the air forces of Egypt, Jordan, and Syria before they could even take to the skies. It was a bold move, one that would define the days to come.

The war on the ground was swift and brutal. In just six days, Israeli forces captured the Gaza Strip and the Sinai Peninsula from Egypt, the West Bank and East Jerusalem from Jordan, and the Golan Heights from Syria. The images of soldiers at the Western Wall, of tanks rolling through the desert, of villages and cities caught in the crossfire. They became etched in the memories of those who saw the war closely.

The aftermath of the war was a mixture of triumph and tragedy. For Israel, it was a moment of unprecedented victory, of securing their homeland against overwhelming odds. But the victory came with a heavy burden. The territories captured during the war brought millions of Palestinians under Israeli control, setting the stage for decades of conflict and negotiations over land and sovereignty.

My education played a significant role in reshaping my perceptions. History classes, books, and discussions introduced me to the complexities of Middle Eastern politics and the deep-rooted animosities that fueled such conflicts. This knowledge did not displace my childhood memories but added layers of understanding to them.

In the years that followed the Six-Day War, the reverberations of the conflict were felt far beyond the immediate aftermath. The war had a profound impact on regional politics. It shattered the prestige of Arab leaders like Nasser and exacerbated tensions between Israel and its neighbors, setting the stage for future conflicts. The sense of invincibility that some Arab nations might have felt was replaced with a desire for revenge and restoration of lost honor, leading eventually to the Yom Kippur War of 1973.

On the international stage, the outcome of the Six-Day War drew global powers even deeper into the Middle East conflict. Both the Soviet Union and the United States found themselves more and more involved, providing diplomatic and military support to their respective allies. This superpower involvement not only heightened the stakes but also made the pursuit of peace more complex and challenging.

For the Palestinian people, the war was a turning point. The territories captured by Israel became central to the Palestinian struggle for statehood, fueling a sense of nationalism and giving rise to movements like the Palestine Liberation Organization (PLO). The displacement of populations and the beginning of the Israeli occupation led to decades of unrest, uprisings, and a continuous cycle of negotiations and conflicts.

As the years turned into decades, the legacy of the Six-Day War continued to influence every facet of life in the region. Peace initiatives came and went, each offering a glimmer of hope that was often eclipsed by new rounds of violence. The war had changed the map, but the deeper battle, the one for understanding, coexistence, and lasting peace, remained.

The decades following the Six-Day War have been characterized by a continuous search for peace amid sporadic outbreaks of conflict. The war's legacy is a dual-edged sword, fostering both resilience and resistance among the people of the region. The territories captured during the war have remained at the heart of the Israeli-Palestinian conflict, a symbol of national aspirations for both sides.

Efforts to resolve the conflict have been numerous, from the Camp David Accords in 1978, which led to a peace treaty between Israel and Egypt, to the Oslo Accords in the 1990s, aimed at achieving a peace agreement between Israel and the Palestinians. Each attempt at peace has underscored the complex historical grievances, security concerns, and political realities that define the region. Despite moments of progress, a lasting resolution has remained elusive, with each side holding onto its deep-seated beliefs and demands.

Yet, amidst the enduring conflict, there have been rays of hope and examples of coexistence. Individuals and organizations from both sides have worked tirelessly to bridge divides, fostering dialogue and understanding through cultural exchanges, joint economic projects, and grassroots peace initiatives. Often overshadowed by the broader conflict, these efforts remind us of the potential for reconciliation and the shared humanity that binds us.

As I reflect on the impact of the Six-Day War and its aftermath, I am reminded of the resilience of the human spirit. Despite the pain and loss, there remains a yearning for peace, a desire to turn the page on a history of conflict and start anew.

However, to acquire that peace, understanding the roots of this conflict is highly important. They are deeply linked to the history, culture, and politics of this region. So, comprehending them requires a journey back through time to events that have shaped the landscape of the Middle East.

I believe that the genesis of this enduring conflict lies in the confluence of two powerful national movements that emerged in the late 19th and early 20th centuries: Zionism and Arab nationalism. Zionism, born out of the Jewish experience of persecution and the dream of returning to their ancestral homeland, and Arab nationalism, rising from the desire for self-determination and independence from colonial rule, were on a collision course that was set against the backdrop of this historically rich and complex land.

My understanding of the conflict deepened with the knowledge of the Balfour Declaration of 1917 and the subsequent British Mandate in Palestine. It was a time of growing Jewish immigration, fueled by the desperate need for a safe haven from European anti-Semitism and the horrors of the Holocaust. Yet, to the Arab inhabitants of Palestine, these developments were seen as a betrayal and a threat to their own aspirations for self-rule and the preservation of their land and identity.

The partition plan of 1947, proposed by the United Nations, was a pivotal moment that I believe could have altered the course of history. The acceptance by the Jewish leadership and the rejection by the Arab side set the stage for the 1948 Arab-Israeli War following the declaration of the State of Israel. The war and those that followed not only reshaped the geopolitical landscape but also sowed seeds of bitterness and grief that have grown deep roots.

From my perspective, the fallout from these conflicts, particularly the displacement of Palestinians and the ongoing occupation, has been a source of enduring pain and resentment. For Israelis, the conflicts have underscored a relentless quest for security in a region where their very right to exist is often challenged. This duality of victimhood and survival, longing for peace and preparing for war, has defined the narratives on both sides.

In my reflections, I have often thought about how the past informs the present. The history of this conflict is not just a list of events; it is a living, breathing legacy that influences every aspect of life here. The checkpoints, the walls, and the news reports of another attack or another round of negotiations carry echoes of the past. They remind us of the deep divisions and the even deeper yearnings for a resolution.

Initiatives like the Camp David Accords and the Oslo Accords, despite their flaws and failings, have shown that dialogue is possible and that peace is not just a dream. Yet, the path to lasting peace is fraught with obstacles, not least of which is the challenge of reconciling these deeply entrenched historical narratives.

However, the way to resolving the conflict demands a delicate balance between remembering and moving forward, between justice and compromise. The Arab-Israeli conflict, with all its historical depth and contemporary implications, continues to teach me the importance of empathy, the value of perspective, and the never-ending quest for a peaceful future.

This ongoing journey through the conflict and attempts at peace has also led me to a deeper appreciation for the human stories behind the headlines. I have listened to narratives from both sides, stories of loss and resilience that transcend the political discourse. These stories have reinforced my belief that at the heart of this conflict are people who, despite their differences, share common aspirations for security, dignity, and a better future for their children.

My reflections on the Arab-Israeli conflict have often been tinged with a sense of frustration at the recurring cycles of violence and missed opportunities for peace. Yet, they are also imbued with an understanding of the complexity of human emotions and the historical burdens that each side carries. The legacy of displacement, the trauma of war, and the fear of existential threats have left deep scars that cannot be ignored in any discussion about peace.

I have come to realize that one of the greatest challenges in resolving this conflict is the need to address not only the political and territorial disputes but also the historical grievances and collective memories that shape each side's identity and position. Acknowledging the pain and suffering of the other without diminishing one's own is a crucial step toward empathy, which I believe is the foundation of any meaningful peace process.

The land of the Middle East, shaped by the contours of its history, tells a story of a land marked by conflict but also by the enduring human spirit. Amidst the despair, there have been moments of hope, instances where individuals and groups from both sides have come together to build bridges of understanding. Though often overshadowed by the broader conflict, these moments remind me that peace is not an unattainable dream but a possibility that requires courage, imagination, and the willingness to see beyond the past.

My story is a testament to the enduring spirit of camaraderie that not even the most profound geopolitical events can sever. As I reflect on the cause and effect of the existing tensions and Arab-Israeli animosity, I am reminded of how our friendship helped ace every obstacle gracefully. In my heart, I hold onto the belief that the day will come when the history of this region will be written not with the ink of conflict but with the colors of reconciliation and peace.

The journey toward this future is long and uncertain, but it is one that we must undertake, armed with the lessons of the past and the hope that our shared humanity will ultimately guide us toward a harmonious coexistence.

Chapter 3: War Drums Beat

"In the Navy, we must always be prepared for the unexpected, for it is in times of crisis that true character is revealed."

- Anonymous.

After a three-day respite in Edinburgh, we prepared to embark on our journey back to Mayport. The prospect of returning home was eagerly anticipated by myself and many of my comrades, including my dear friends Steve and Philip. Having been away since April 1973, we were determined to make it back in time for Thanksgiving and Christmas, excited to participate in the festivities with our families.

During our time at sea, Philip Milton, Steve Hargis, and I forged a profound bond that would endure for years to come. With his years of experience and seasoned knowledge, Milton became a leading force in the Navy. He made wise decisions and provided his fellow sailors with important support. His quick thinking would later prove life-saving when the Belknap collided with the Kennedy during our subsequent cruise. On the other hand, Hargis possessed a laid-back demeanor but showcased unparalleled skill as an Aviation Fire Control Technician. This earned him a reputation as one of the finest in his field.

Philip would have liked to explore Edinburgh with Steve and me, but he was obligated to the ship to perform duty watch. During the Yom Kippur War, which could aptly be dubbed the "Secret War" from my perspective, we were privy to scant information about the broader context. As we were on duty, we only received our daily directives and immediate mission details.

At the young age of twenty-two, there was little room for questioning military commands; obedience was the expected norm.

Compliance with military orders was mandatory; questioning them was a luxury we could not afford. As the Kennedy departed from Edinburgh, we had yet to officially integrate into the sixth fleet. Operation Nickel Grass had not commenced, positioning us to aid in the critical transfer of aircraft to Israel. It was not until the 25th of October that we reunited with the sixth fleet in the Mediterranean, alongside two other aircraft carriers, poised to assert control over the airspace.

In the United States Navy, an officer is a commissioned military personnel. During the Yom Kippur War, I was an E-5 petty officer in the US Navy and was ensnared in secrecy and haste. President Richard Nixon's policy of détente, which intended to ease tensions between the United States and the Soviet Union, failed spectacularly in the face of the Middle Eastern conflict. Instead of soothing international relations, it ignited an inferno that threatened to engulf the entire region in flames.

Caught in the crossfire were Israel, Egypt, Syria, and their respective allies, teetering on the precipice of a nuclear confrontation. As the United States upgraded its defense readiness condition to Defcon 3, the entire world held its breath. It was a sobering reminder of how serious the situation was. Despite the frightening escalation, the Soviet Union eventually abandoned its confrontational stance. This averted catastrophe left damaged diplomatic relations.

The important decision that President Nixon made to back Israel during this dangerous period has political, moral, and geopolitical ramifications. Created under intense Cold War competition, it was a risk with serious consequences. Some praised it as a daring show of support for a steadfast ally, while others denounced it as irresponsible brinkmanship that would only heighten tensions in an already unstable area.

Operation Nickel Grass, however, was a ray of glee that appeared amid the confusion and uncertainty. This clandestine operation, led by the US Air Force, was to restock Israel with essential supplies and weaponry in an effort to shift the balance of power in their favor. I participated in this covert operation as an officer tasked with carrying out my superiors' commands.

The United States Navy was prepared to provide Operation Nickel Grass with unmatched firepower thanks to its impressive inventory of cutting-edge planes and cutting-edge technologies. We flew over the Mediterranean Sea, watching over the airspace, courageously deploying supplies to the beleaguered country.

For me, the conflict resembled a closely held secret, a murky place where honor and duty collided with risk and uncertainty. Each assignment came with a heavy burden of accountability and the understanding that failure was not an option. I had a strong sense of purpose and a resolve to see the mission through to a successful end.

In the end, Operation Nickel Grass proved to be a turning point in the conflict, a demonstration of the indomitable spirit of courage and resilience. The people of Israel stood united in the face of hardship, refusing to give up even when the cards were stacked against them. Even while war wounds might never completely heal, they serve as a constant reminder of the costs incurred for the sake of justice and freedom.

I couldn't help but think back on the turbulent events that had transpired as the dust settled and the sounds of the conflict vanished from my mind. Although President Nixon's choice to back Israel was contentious at the time, it was ultimately motivated by a strong sense of conviction and steadfast resolve. And despite the uncertain path ahead, I'm firm in my resolve to stand out for the principles that make our country what it is. Because it is in the furnace of war that great heroes are made, and their acts are immortalized in the pages of history.

The Yom Kippur War aftermath permanently altered the geopolitical environment. It changed the Middle East's power dynamics, reshaping alliances. One thing was quite evident when the battle passed, and the world assessed the destruction caused by it: Operation Nickel Grass's lasting legacy.

Some saw it as little more than a historical footnote, eclipsed by the flashy diplomacy and larger-than-life figures, but others saw its critical role in determining how the war turned out. Operation Nickel Grass was more than just a military operation. In my opinion, it was also a monument to the strength of will and the resilience of the human spirit.

I am reminded of the heroic men and women who gave their lives to secure the mission's success as I think back on those turbulent days. All of them contributed significantly to the final victory, from the pilots who made risky missions well into enemy territory to the ground crews who gave their all to keep our planes in the air.

Since we were away from home, we, too, were the heroes among all of them. For me, as for every other soldier, home has always been the most valuable thing. I have a particular place in my heart for it. More significantly, though, home is a symbol of tranquility and hope. I can live the life I have always wanted in this place. Even with all of the struggles I had while serving in the Marines, I never gave up hope that one day I would return home, leaving the harsh waters behind and sinking into the warmth of my surroundings.

As much as I craved my home, I was always up to serve the orders I received. There was a noticeable disappointment in the air as word of our prolonged deployment traveled across the ship. A lot of us had been looking forward to Thanksgiving so we could enjoy the warmth and cheer of the season with our family. It appeared that fate had another plan for us.

The tone on board was depressing for days as we struggled to accept the truth of our circumstances. Worry and doubt etched faces that had once been radiant with anticipation. Nevertheless, despite our dismay, our crew possessed a quiet tenacity that ran throughout.

After all, we were sailors bound by duty and honor to serve our country with pride and dedication. And even though we were quite concerned about missing Thanksgiving, we understood that our goal was the most important thing. We resolved to finish the task at hand, so we put aside our personal wants and concentrated on it.

In the end, our extended deployment proved to be a test of our resilience and fortitude, a reminder of the sacrifices we were willing to make in service to our country. With our hearts full of hope and expectation, we knew that no matter what obstacles lay ahead, we would overcome them as a crew, one in purpose and commitment. This was evident as we sped toward home. Even though the voyage was lengthy and difficult, the friendships and memories we formed would last a lifetime.

Chapter 4: Gearing Up for Conflict

"The supreme art of war is to subdue the enemy without fighting."

- Sun Tzu

President Richard Nixon attempted a different strategy amid the Cold War, one that was based on the desire to calm the turbulent geopolitics. He called it détente, a French word for easing tensions, and aimed to soften the hard lines dividing the United States from the Soviet Union. Yet, when the Yom Kippur War erupted, it tested the resilience of U.S.–Soviet relations to their limits, bringing the two superpowers perilously close to confrontation. This period did not showcase détente's strength; rather, it revealed its fragility under pressure.

The administrations of Syria and Egypt harbored doubts about Nixon's dedication to this policy, especially regarding its application in the Middle East. They perceived an imbalance, feeling that the United States had tilted too favorably toward Israel. This skepticism underscored a broader challenge: maintaining a policy of détente required more than just declarations; it demanded tangible actions that all parties could interpret as fair and balanced. Unfortunately, in the cauldron of Middle Eastern politics, achieving such equilibrium proved elusive.

In the autumn of 1973, when the Yom Kippur War unfolded, the United States Navy, particularly the 6th Fleet, emerged as a basis of support for Israel in its moment of dire need against the combined might of Egyptian and Syrian forces. A nation's fortitude and resiliency were tested during this period of strained alliances and geopolitical maneuvering.

The United States didn't just stand by; it actively participated in reinforcing Israel's defense capabilities. The provision of logistical support was a lifeline for Israel, encompassing a wide range of essentials from ammunition and spare parts to aircraft. These supplies were not merely items on a checklist but were the very sinews that allowed Israel to sustain its military endeavors during this pivotal conflict.

Moreover, the sharing of intelligence between the United States and Israel went beyond the formalities of alliance; it was a proof of trust and strategic cooperation. The insights into Egyptian and Syrian plans and movements were not just data— they were the eyes through which Israel could anticipate and steer the storm of warfare. Even when the choice was made to hold back on immediate military response, the value of this shared knowledge was undeniable.

One of the most notable undertakings was the airlift operations. Under the guise of Operation Nickel Grass, the U.S. Air Force undertook a mammoth task of transporting critical military equipment and supplies across continents to Israel's doorstep. These operations were the arteries pumping vital support, ensuring that the pulse of Israel's defense forces never waned.

The U.S. Navy's role, though covered in secrecy at the time, was no less significant. The Navy was the silent guardian, ensuring that aid reached its target without hindrance by refueling planes, securing the airspace, and establishing authority over the Mediterranean.

Beyond the battleground, the United States also played a crucial role on the diplomatic front. Its assistance went beyond tactical and material support and into the sphere of international diplomacy, assisting Israel in obtaining the support required to confront not only current dangers but even more significant issues on the world scene.

The constant vigil of the U.S. 6th Fleet in the Mediterranean served as a stark warning to anyone who might contemplate disrupting this flow of support. Their presence was a shield, not just in the literal sense, but as a symbol of support, reassuring Israel and contributing to a semblance of stability in a region rocked by conflict.

As one who has observed the ripples of these actions across time, it's clear that the partnership between the United States and Israel during those fraught weeks was not merely a chapter in military strategy but a reflection of deep-seated alliances and the enduring spirit of cooperation in the face of adversity.

The foundation of the operational readiness of the United States Navy is a demanding and comprehensive training program. With an emphasis on preparing its sailors for the demands of combat, the Navy has developed a comprehensive approach to training. This technique encompasses more than just weapon proficiency and physical stamina; it also involves technical proficiency, mental acuity, and the kind of discipline that can only be developed through intense training. From the moment a recruit steps into boot camp, they begin a journey that is as much about personal transformation as it is about acquiring the skills necessary for survival and effectiveness in diverse operational theaters.

At the very foundation of this journey is Basic Training, where the raw material of potential is shaped into the steel of naval capability. After these first few weeks, sailors attend specialized training institutions where the emphasis is on the particular duties they will play inside the Navy's massive apparatus. The learning curve does not plateau with the completion of this phase; instead, it continues to ascend through ongoing education and opportunities for advancement. This perpetual cycle of learning ensures that the Navy not only keeps pace with the evolving nature of maritime warfare but often stays several steps ahead.

Collaboration extends beyond the confines of the United States Navy, reaching across borders to allies and partners under the NATO umbrella. Together, they confront the myriad challenges that threaten maritime security—from the specter of piracy on the high seas to the clandestine movements of illegal trafficking and the operations of terrorism.

These collaborations are manifested in joint patrols that cut silent swathes through the ocean, in the shared intelligence that might prevent the next crisis, and in the collective strengthening of capabilities that underpin these efforts.

Such international cooperation was vividly demonstrated before the USS John F Kennedy and its consorts arrived in Edinburgh, Scotland. They had just concluded their participation in "Swift Move," a NATO-led exercise of considerable scale.

Designed to test and enhance the alliance's rapid deployment capabilities, this exercise simulated the kind of crisis scenario that demands swift, coordinated action. It underscored not just the Navy's readiness to respond to potential threats but also its commitment to collective security efforts that span the North Atlantic. This enhanced the peace and stability in an area essential to the security of the entire world.

The United States Navy provides an example of its undying commitment to quality and readiness through this combination of rigorous training, continuing education, and international cooperation. It's evidence for the idea that a navy's power comes from its sailors' tenacity, ability, and friendship as much as from the steel of its vessels.

Amid the evolving global tableau of the early 1970s, marked notably by the outbreak of the Yom Kippur War, the foundational ethos and readiness of the United States Navy were subtly but indelibly tested.

The unexpected escalation of hostilities in the Middle East, resulting from the concerted attack on Israel by Egyptian and Syrian forces, necessitated a recalibration of the principles that underpin the Navy's doctrine: rigorous training, continuous education, and international cooperation. At this point, the essence of naval strength was emphasized, stressing not only the fleet's physical strength but also—and perhaps more importantly—the readiness, adaptability, and esprit de corps of its sailors. The unplanned extension of John F. Kennedy's stay in Edinburgh, in this case, went beyond a straightforward detour from the schedule.

John F. Kennedy, initially destined for a brief sojourn in Edinburgh, extended her stay due to unforeseen circumstances. It was in the autumn of 1973, amid the changing leaves and the cooling air, that another chapter of tension unfolded in the Middle East. Egyptian and Syrian forces, in a sudden and bold move, initiated an attack on Israel on the 6th of October, marking the beginning of the Yom Kippur War. This event prompted a swift and strategic response.

That being said, on October 13, Kennedy, the guided missile destroyer Richard E. Byrd, the destroyer Sarsfield, and the oiler Caloosahatchee made their way out of Edinburgh. Their destination was a strategic point 100 miles west of Gibraltar, where they assumed a vigilant stance, ready to respond to the escalating crisis.

The days passed, each bringing its own set of challenges and developments. On the 25th of October, a significant turn of events came just after the A-4 Skyhawks had successfully been flown to Israel, making their journey through the Azores and joining forces with Franklin D. Roosevelt, which was positioned south of Sicily. It was then that John F. Kennedy received orders that would bring her back into the fold of the 6th Fleet, guiding her into the Mediterranean Sea.

The situation was fraught with tension, not just on the battlegrounds but also on the geopolitical chessboard. Reports had emerged of the Soviet Union's intentions to deploy troops into the Middle East, ostensibly to oversee the fragile ceasefire that had been established between Israel and its neighbors.

This development prompted a heightened state of alert for U.S. forces globally. In the midst of this, John F. Kennedy readied herself, preparing contingency weapons loads on the 27th of October, standing by for any eventuality.

This period was proof of the unpredictability of international affairs, where plans could change as swiftly as the winds and where the preparedness and resolve of those involved were continually tested.

Chapter 5: Passage to Peril

"In war, truth is the first casualty."

- Aeschylus

The war commenced on Yom Kippur, the holiest day in the Jewish calendar, exploiting Israel's moment of reflection and prayer for an unexpected military advantage. This timing reflected a pre-planned strategy by Egypt and Syria, aiming to reclaim territories lost to Israel during the 1967 Six-Day War.

The initial phase of the war delivered a stark blow to Israel. Egyptian and Syrian forces launched simultaneous attacks across the Sinai Peninsula and the Golan Heights, respectively. This offensive caught Israel off-guard, stretching its military thin and inflicting substantial material and human losses. The surprise element of the attack put Israel in a precarious position, requiring rapid adaptation and strategic recalibration.

The United States, observing the unfolding situation with concern, recognized the critical need to support its ally. Despite its official stance of neutrality, the U.S. played a crucial role in aiding Israel's recovery efforts through significant military support, thereby reinforcing the strategic partnership between the two nations.

The lead-up to the Yom Kippur War was characterized by a complex geopolitics in the Middle East, marked by persistent tensions and the aftermath of previous conflicts between Israel and its Arab neighbors. The 1967 Six-Day War had significantly altered the region's territorial boundaries, leaving Egypt and

Syria seeking an opportunity to recapture lost lands and restore their national pride. The planning and execution of the Yom Kippur attack were rooted in these motivations, with both countries aiming to challenge Israel's military superiority and alter the regional power balance.

The selection of Yom Kippur for the attack was not coincidental. Egypt and Syria anticipated that Israel's state of reduced vigilance during the day of atonement would provide a tactical advantage. This assumption proved correct initially, as the surprise attack disrupted the usual rhythm of Israeli life and its military's preparedness. The timing of the assault, leveraging a period of religious observance, underscored the depth of strategic planning undertaken by the Arab coalition. It was a move designed to maximize the impact of their military initiative and regain the initiative in the Arab-Israeli conflict.

As the war progressed, the initial shock of the surprise attack began to dissipate. Israel, with the aid of the United States, swiftly mobilized its resources and counterattacked. This rapid response demonstrated Israel's resilience and the critical role of U.S. support in facilitating its recovery. The war, while a moment of significant challenge for Israel, also underscored the enduring strategic partnership between Israel and the United States. This alliance would prove instrumental in the conflict's subsequent phases, as Israel sought to reverse the early gains made by Egypt and Syria and secure its position in a volatile region.

The Battle of the Sinai Peninsula commenced as Egyptian forces launched a well-coordinated assault, exploiting the element of surprise against an unprepared Israeli defense. Utilizing modern anti-tank weapons and infantry tactics, Egyptian troops managed to breach the formidable Bar-Lev Line, a chain of fortifications along the eastern bank of the Suez Canal, which was thought to be impenetrable. The initial success of this offensive stunned the Israeli military, prompting a critical reassessment of their defensive and retaliatory strategies.

Simultaneously, the northern front witnessed the outbreak of the Battle of the Golan Heights. Syrian forces, armed with the ambition of recapturing territory lost during the Six-Day War of 1967, initiated a multi-pronged attack against Israeli positions.

Despite facing a terrain advantageous to the defenders and a numerically superior enemy, the Syrians made significant initial gains, underscoring the effectiveness of their surprise attack and the intensity of their preparation. It not only allowed the Arab coalitions to gain early momentum but also exposed vulnerabilities within the Israeli military strategy and preparedness. However, the tide of the war began to shift as Israel regrouped and initiated counterattacks.

Israel's response to the unfolding crisis was marked by a swift mobilization of reserves and a reconfiguration of its military tactics. In the Sinai, counteroffensives were launched to stem the Egyptian advance, characterized by a combination of air superiority and ground maneuvers that aimed to encircle and isolate the advancing Egyptian units. These operations gradually eroded the initial gains made by Egypt, demonstrating the resilience and adaptability of the Israeli forces under pressure.

On the Golan Heights, the situation was dire, with Syrian forces threatening to break through to the heart of northern Israel. The response was proof of Israel's determination to reverse the course of the conflict. Reinforcements were rushed to the front, and through a series of fierce engagements, Israeli forces managed to halt the Syrian advance. The counteroffensive that followed pushed Syrian troops back, securing the Golan Heights and restoring a defensive stance that would persist for the remainder of the war.

Israel's ability to recover from the initial shocks of the conflict and launch effective counterattacks was pivotal. It not only demonstrated the importance of quick adaptation and the effective mobilization of reserve forces but also highlighted the critical role of intelligence, airpower, and combined arms operations in modern warfare. These battles did not just influence the immediate outcome of the war; they also contributed to a broader understanding of the military dynamics in the region, shaping future conflicts and peace negotiations.

In the thick of the 1973 Yom Kippur War, Operation Nickel Grass emerged as a crucial U.S. initiative, underpinning the strategic airlift of military supplies to Israel. Conceived during a time of escalated hostilities, this operation highlighted the material expression of American assistance to Israel. It maneuvered through a convoluted geopolitics characterized by tensions from the Cold War and the Arab-Israeli conflict.

Operation Nickel Grass was initiated in response to a critical juncture in the war, as Israel faced a surprise attack from a coalition of Arab states led by Egypt and Syria. The operation aimed to replenish Israel's dwindling military supplies, ensuring its armed forces could continue to defend their nation against the multifront offensive.

The initial surprise attack on Israel caught both the United States and Israel off guard, accelerating the war's progression. However, with substantial support from the United States, Israel quickly regrouped. Throughout the conflict, specific battles and incidents played critical roles, potentially influencing the war's outcome. Egypt and Syria's attacks resulted in considerable casualties and material losses. Yet, the element of surprise merely postponed Israel's ability to organize a rapid counteroffensive.

The sudden attack initially shocked Israel, but they managed to regroup and respond effectively with significant support from the United States. This attack merely postponed their retaliation until they could deploy their military reserves.

The United States, leveraging its Military Airlift Command, mobilized a fleet of C-5 Galaxy and C-141 Starlifter cargo aircraft. These planes, renowned for their substantial payload capacities, were tasked with transporting essential weapons, ammunition, and military equipment directly to Israel.

However, the operation was not without its challenges. A significant hurdle emerged as several European countries, wary of jeopardizing their diplomatic relations with the Arab states and possibly inciting economic repercussions, notably the oil embargo, refused the U.S. aircraft access to their airspace and refueling facilities.

A pivotal solution to this logistical quandary was the utilization of Lajes Field in the Azores for refueling. This Portuguese archipelago, strategically located in the North Atlantic Ocean, became an indispensable waypoint for the

American airlift. The operation's inventiveness and flexibility were demonstrated by the construction of a makeshift air bridge across Lajes Field. It enabled the cargo planes to get around European limitations and continue providing Israel with military assistance.

The impact of Operation Nickel Grass on the war's dynamics was profound. Israel's defense capabilities were significantly strengthened by the prompt delivery of U.S. military supplies, which allowed it to offset the early victories of the troops in Egypt and Syria. More than just a military lifeline, the operation signified a deeper affirmation of the strategic partnership between the United States and Israel. It was a clear demonstration of America's commitment to Israel's security and sovereignty, transcending mere diplomatic support to manifest in substantial, on-the-ground aid.

Similarly, Operation Nickel Grass had broader implications beyond the immediate military benefits it provided. It underscored the geopolitical significance of U.S.-Israel relations within the context of the Cold War, serving as a counterbalance to the Soviet Union's support for the Arab states. The operation not only facilitated a pivotal shift in the war's momentum in favor of Israel but also reinforced the United States' position as a dominant player in Middle Eastern politics.

As the tensions heightened, the Mediterranean Sea witnessed a significant show of American naval strength. The deployment of the USS John F. Kennedy, USS Franklin D. Roosevelt, and USS Independence served as a clear message, not just to the combatants but to the entire international community. These formidable naval assets, representing the United States Sixth

Fleet, held positions with strategic finesse, signaling support for Israel while carefully dealing with Cold War politics and detente.

The presence of these aircraft carriers and their accompanying fleets provided a multifaceted advantage. For Israel, reeling from the surprise attacks by Egypt and Syria, the sight and knowledge of American naval power nearby offered substantial reassurance. It bolstered the morale of the Israeli forces and populace, reminding them that they were not alone in their struggle for survival against an enemy coalition determined to redraw the map of the Middle East.

Conversely, for the Arab coalition, the proximity of such an overwhelming naval force served as a deterrent against further escalation of the conflict. The implicit threat posed by these carriers and their capacity to project American military might onto any theater of operations in the region was a cautionary tale. It arguably prevented the conflict from expanding, sparing the region from what could have escalated into a far more devastating war.

Similarly, the strategic positioning of these naval assets provided the United States with diplomatic leverage and flexibility. At a time when the global balance of power was delicately poised between the superpowers of the United States and the Soviet Union, the Sixth Fleet's presence was a tangible representation of American interests and intentions in the Mediterranean. It allowed the Nixon administration to exert influence in negotiations, striving for a ceasefire while maintaining neutrality dictated by its detente policy with the Soviet Union.

While publicly adhering to neutrality, the U.S. was, in reality, deeply committed to ensuring Israel's survival and eventual victory. This dual strategy presented a diplomatic tightrope walk as the administration sought to balance its support for Israel with the need to avoid provoking a direct confrontation with the Soviet Union, which was backing the Arab states.

The United States' military strategy and ties with the Soviet Union were affected more broadly by this sophisticated approach. On the one hand, the airlift operation codenamed Nickel Grass, which saw the United States resupply Israel with arms and ammunition, underscored the extent of U.S. commitment to Israel's defense. On the other hand, the careful management of the Sixth Fleet's role demonstrated a strategic restraint designed to keep the conflict from spiraling into a superpower confrontation.

Later, the conflict, which saw Israel fiercely opposed by the combined forces of Egypt and Syria, ended without a decisive victor, but its aftermath laid the groundwork for future diplomatic and military developments in the region. For Israel, Egypt, Syria, and their neighbors, the war's conclusion marked a period of reassessment and realignment, compelling each to adapt to a new status quo.

Israel, having been caught off-guard by the surprise attacks on Yom Kippur, the holiest day in the Jewish calendar, found itself reevaluating its military and strategic approaches. The initial successes of Egypt and Syria in breaching Israeli defenses underscored vulnerabilities that Israel had previously overlooked. This insight led to a thorough review of Israel's military preparedness and intelligence-gathering capabilities. It enabled more efficient foreseeing and neutralization of potential threats. Furthermore, the war emphasized the critical importance of technological superiority and adaptable tactics in modern warfare, lessons that Israel would integrate into its defense doctrine.

One of the most significant outcomes of the war was the cementing of the alliance between the United States and Israel. The U.S. played an indispensable role in Israel's ability to withstand and ultimately counter the Arab offensive, primarily through Operation Nickel Grass, a strategic airlift that provided Israel with the military supplies necessary to continue fighting. This operation not only demonstrated the logistical capabilities of the U.S. Military Airlift Command but also highlighted the strategic depth of the U.S.-Israel relationship.

The presence of American naval forces in the Mediterranean served as both a psychological boost to Israeli morale and a deterrent to further escalation by Arab states or Soviet intervention. This alliance, strengthened in the crucible of conflict, would evolve into a cornerstone of U.S. foreign policy in the Middle East, characterized by ongoing military support and cooperation.

The Yom Kippur War's conclusion also prompted a broader reflection on the path to peace in the Middle East. The conflict underscored the unsustainable nature of perpetual warfare in the region and the necessity of diplomatic engagement. In the years following the war, efforts to negotiate peace between Israel and its neighbors gained momentum, leading to historic agreements like the Camp David Accords. These negotiations, though fraught with challenges, represented a shift toward recognizing the need for coexistence and mutual security arrangements.

The war not only tested Israel's resilience and military prowess but also underscored the indispensability of international support, particularly from the United States, in ensuring the nation's survival. The conflict catalyzed a reassessment of military strategies and alliances, which, in turn, influenced the regional balance of power and the pursuit of peace. As the dust settled, the legacy of the war served as a stark reminder of the complexities of the Middle East conflict and the enduring quest for stability and peace in a region all too familiar with the ravages of war.

Chapter 6: Baptism by Fire

As the Yom Kippur War unfolded, the Sixth Fleet found itself in the eye of the storm, not just monitoring the conflict but actively preparing to respond to any escalation that might threaten the delicate balance in the region. This wasn't just another mission. For the sailors and officers aboard the USS Independence, the USS Franklin D. Roosevelt, and the USS John F. Kennedy, it was a test of their readiness and resolve in the face of an unpredictable and volatile situation.

While the world's eyes were fixed on the battles raging on the Golan Heights and the Suez Canal, the Sixth Fleet served as a silent guardian, a keeper of the peace in waters that had become a chessboard for superpower rivalry. It was a role that demanded not just military might but also a deep understanding of the region's complex politics and history.

For many of the men and women who served in the Sixth Fleet, the Yom Kippur War was a defining moment in their careers. They were not just witnesses to history; they were participants in a broader story of conflict, diplomacy, and the endless quest for peace in a region where history is measured not just in years but in millennia.

As we dig into the details of the fleet's mission, the strategic importance of its presence, and the personal experiences of those who stood watch over the Mediterranean, we gain a full understanding of the indispensable role played by naval power in shaping the outcomes of global conflicts.

Amidst the ongoing war, the U.S. Sixth Fleet, stationed in the Mediterranean Sea, had its hands full. Their main job was to keep an eye on the conflict, ensuring that American interests and allies in the region stayed safe. The Sixth Fleet stepped in to help with peace talks, and they were there for the U.S. allies, especially Israel. They shared important intelligence, helped with logistical needs, and were ready to step in militarily if things got worse.

They also played a big part in trying to keep things calm in the Mediterranean, stopping potential threats in their tracks and showing the U.S.'s commitment to keeping its friends and interests safe in the Middle East. From October 14 to November 15, 1973, the Sixth Fleet's air teams were busy. They flew combat air patrols to keep the airlifts safe and to prepare for the arrival of new A4 Skyhawks. During these flights, every squadron had to have Flight Deck Troubleshooters ready to go. I was in VA-46, and they needed me to take on this crucial job, though I was initially hesitant.

It's tricky to say for sure how using different U.S. planes like the A-7 Corsairs and F-4 Phantoms might have changed the outcome of the Yom Kippur War. The A-7s were definitely an upgrade with their better tech and capabilities compared to the A-4 Skyhawks. And the F-4 Phantoms? They were top-notch for air battles.

The war was complicated, with so many things happening at once. Everything from surprise attacks by Egypt and Syria to how well Israel could defend and strike back to the efforts from around the world to bring peace played a part in how things turned out. If the U.S. had provided Israel with these more advanced planes, it might have given them an edge, with better air defense and stronger attacks, thanks to the cutting-edge systems on these aircraft.

This demonstration of commitment was linked to the broader objectives of U.S. foreign policy. The Sixth Fleet's presence in the Mediterranean was a piece of a larger puzzle, aiming to maintain a balance in the region that favored peace over escalation. During the Cold War, with the Soviet Union eyeing the conflict with keen interest, the fleet's role in deterring aggression took on added significance.

All in all, even though these advanced planes might have made a difference, the war's outcome hinged on a whole lot of complicated factors that went way beyond just the specs of the aircraft used. Strategically, the Yom Kippur War played a critical role in a complicated geopolitical chess game, where each move was carefully calculated to avoid provoking further hostilities while ensuring the region remained stable. The fleet's operations were a clear signal to friends and foes alike that the United States was deeply invested in the security of the Middle East.

Yet, beyond the grand strategy and high-stakes diplomacy, there was a personal element to the Sixth Fleet's mission. For the sailors aboard those ships, the Mediterranean was not just a theater of operations but a place where they witnessed history unfolding. They understood the gravity of their mission and the impact of their presence. It was a moment in time where the professional and the personal intersected, where the task of monitoring a distant conflict became linked with the stories of individuals committed to a cause greater than themselves.

As the war unfolded, the Mediterranean Sea was a chessboard of naval power, where the United States' Sixth Fleet played a dominant role in overseeing the volatile situation. Central to this effort were three giant steel sentinels: the USS Independence (CV-62), the USS Franklin D. Roosevelt (CV-42), and the USS John F. Kennedy (CV-67). These carrier groups were not just floating airbases but symbols of American commitment to peace and security in the region.

The USS Independence, a Forrestal-class aircraft carrier, was the flagship of the Sixth Fleet during this period. Its presence in the Mediterranean was a clear signal of the U.S.'s readiness to respond to any threat. Alongside the Independence, Franklin D. Roosevelt, another Forrestal-class carrier, added its formidable capabilities to the fleet. Completing this trio was the USS John F. Kennedy, a Kitty Hawk-class carrier, which joined the Sixth Fleet later in October, each bringing its unique story and crew to the forefront of this naval endeavor.

The role of these carrier groups extended far beyond mere symbols of power. They were tasked with a range of missions critical to the success of the Sixth Fleet's objectives. Air support was paramount, with their squadrons ready to take to the skies at a moment's notice to defend allied forces and interests. Reconnaissance flights were routine, gathering vital intelligence that would shape the strategic decisions of commanders. Beyond this, the carriers were instruments of power projection. Their very presence acted as a deterrent to hostile actions, while their capability to launch a wide range of offensive operations stood as a testament to their versatility on the open sea.

Supporting these giants of the sea were many escorting ships, each increasing the naval power projection. With their advanced radar and missile systems, cruisers served as the fleet's protective shield, ready to intercept any threat. Destroyers, agile and deadly, patrolled the waters, ensuring the safety of the carriers and the broader fleet from submarine and surface threats. Submarines, silent and unseen, added an extra layer of deterrence, making adversaries think twice before making any aggressive moves.

This armada was more than just a collection of ships; it was a floating community, a tight-knit family of sailors and aviators bonded by the mission and the challenges they faced together. Life on these carriers was a blend of routine and adrenaline, where moments of calm were often broken by the roar of jet engines taking off on another mission. It was a world where professionalism met personal sacrifice, as each member of the fleet knew the importance of their role.

Fighter Squadrons stood as the guardians of the Fleet. Flying the formidable F-4 Phantom II, these units specialized in air superiority and defense. Pilots and their crews trained for countless hours to master the skies, ready to confront any aerial threat. Their mission was not just to protect the Fleet but to ensure dominance in the airspace over the eastern Mediterranean. With its speed and firepower, the Phantom II was an ideal aircraft for this task, equipped with air-to-air missiles that could engage enemy aircraft from a distance.

Attack Squadrons, on the other hand, were the Fleet's long arm, capable of striking targets far beyond the horizon. Flying the A-7 Corsair II and the A-6 Intruder, these units specialized in ground attacks and precision strikes. Their missions were risky, often flying into heavily defended areas to hit strategic targets. These squadrons were essential in demonstrating the Fleet's ability to project power ashore, supporting allied forces and disrupting enemy operations.

Reconnaissance Squadrons played the eyes of the Fleet. Operating aircraft like the RF-8 Crusader and the RA-5C Vigilante, they undertook high-speed, high-altitude missions over enemy territory, gathering critical intelligence. In a time without satellites or drones, these missions were crucial for collecting real-time data on enemy movements and vulnerabilities.

Early Warning and Electronic Warfare squadrons were the unsung heroes, providing an electronic shield around the Fleet and its allies. Operating the E-2 Hawkeye and the EA-6B Prowler, they offered a dual capability: detecting enemy aircraft and missiles from afar and jamming enemy radar and communications. Their work often went unnoticed but was vital in ensuring the Fleet's operations remained hidden from prying eyes and that allied aircraft could operate without fear of enemy air defenses.

In the context of the Yom Kippur War, the diverse capabilities of these squadrons were not just a show of force but a strategic necessity. They ensured the Sixth Fleet could monitor the conflict, support U.S. policy objectives, and deter aggression in a volatile region. The operations conducted by these squadrons went beyond mere military might; they demonstrated a commitment to stability and security in the Mediterranean, reassuring allies and deterring foes. With its unique capabilities, each squadron contributed to a multifaceted strategy that extended American influence and safeguarded interests in a critical part of the world.

The A-7B Corsair II, a workhorse of ground attack missions, was known for its ability to carry a wide range of munitions. This versatile aircraft could be armed with a variety of bombs, both guided and unguided, making it a formidable tool for precision strikes. General-purpose bombs like the MK 82 and MK 83 were staples in its arsenal, complemented by cluster bombs for area targets and laser-guided bombs for pinpoint accuracy. Its capability to carry air-to-ground missiles, such as the AGM-65 Maverick, further enhanced its role in striking armored targets with precision, while its rocket pods added another layer of versatility to its ground attack capabilities.

Equally impressive was the F-4 Phantom II, a symbol of air superiority that patrolled the skies with vigilance. Armed with air-to-air missiles like the AIM-7 Sparrow and the AIM-9 Sidewinder, the Phantom was a predator, ready to engage enemy aircraft in lethal combat. Its adaptability in carrying a range of missiles allowed it to dominate air-to-air engagements and maintain control of the airspace over the fleet.

These aircraft were not just platforms for weapons; they were extensions of the strategic thinking that underpinned the Sixth Fleet's operations. The selection of munitions was a testament to the emphasis on versatility and precision. The ability to choose the right weapon for the right target meant that the Sixth Fleet could effectively engage a variety of threats, from ground installations to enemy fighters, ensuring that its presence was felt across the battlefield.

The strategic implications of these weaponry choices were profound. Precision strikes enabled by the A-7B's varied munitions could cripple enemy defenses and support ground operations without putting troops at unnecessary risk. Meanwhile, the air superiority secured by the F-4 Phantom II's missiles ensured that the Sixth Fleet's operations could proceed without the threat of enemy air interference. Together, these aircraft and their munitions played a pivotal role in projecting power and maintaining stability in a region on the edge.

As the conflict unfolded, the Sixth Fleet's use of these advanced weapons systems underscored the importance of technological superiority in modern warfare. The ability to strike with precision, to choose from a diverse arsenal tailored to specific mission needs, and to control the skies above were not just tactical advantages. They were clear messages to friends and foes alike of the commitment and capability of the United States to defend its interests and support its allies.

One could imagine the tension aboard these carriers, where pilots and crew worked around the clock. There was a constant hum of activity as aircraft were launched and recovered, missions briefed and debriefed. Amidst this, there were moments of anticipation as the fleet received updates on the war's progress and relief, and missions returned successfully.

Despite its might and preparedness, the Sixth Fleet's direct engagement in the conflict was measured. Its primary role was deterrence and support, proof of the delicate balance of power and the need to avoid escalating the conflict further. Yet, the fleet's presence had a significant psychological impact. It served as a stern warning to other actors in the region, deterring potential aggression against U.S. allies and interests.

The effectiveness of the Sixth Fleet in fulfilling its mission objectives during the Yom Kippur War was multifaceted. It did not engage directly in battle but provided critical support that contributed to the stability of the region. Its capabilities in air warfare and reconnaissance ensured that U.S. allies felt less isolated, knowing that a powerful friend was just over the horizon, ready to come to their aid if the tide turned.

As the conflict came to an end and negotiations began, the role of the Sixth Fleet in ensuring a balance of power and providing a visible sign of U.S. commitment to the region's stability was widely acknowledged. It was a quiet force during the storm of war, always ready but restrained, a guardian of peace in uncertain times.

However, the operations of the Sixth Fleet in those turbulent times left an indelible mark on U.S. military strategy in the Mediterranean. The region, a crossroads of geopolitical interests, saw an increased U.S. naval presence as a direct consequence of the fleet's successful mission. This reinforced presence served as a deterrent to potential aggressors and underscored America's commitment to safeguarding its interests and those of its allies. The Sixth Fleet's actions during the Yom Kippur War underscored the importance of a strong naval force in maintaining stability and peace in global hotspots.

The lessons learned from the 1973 conflict were profound. They highlighted the critical importance of readiness, flexibility, and the ability to project power across the seas. Future naval operations would draw upon these lessons, emphasizing the need for a fleet to respond swiftly to emerging threats and operate effectively in a complex globe. The Sixth Fleet's experience during the Yom Kippur War informed strategies that prioritized rapid deployment capabilities, advanced reconnaissance, and the integration of new technologies to enhance the fleet's operational effectiveness.

The narrative of the Sixth Fleet during the Yom Kippur War might be viewed as a monument to the U.S. Navy's tenacity and strength. It serves as a reminder of the critical role that naval forces play in protecting national interests and promoting global stability. The operations of the Sixth Fleet not only demonstrated the United States' commitment to its allies but also set the stage for future naval strategies that prioritize readiness, flexibility, and technological superiority. Looking back, it's clear that the experiences of the Sixth Fleet in 1973 have shaped the course of naval operations, ensuring that the fleet remains a cornerstone of U.S. military strategy in the Mediterranean and beyond.

Chapter 7: The Strategic Airlift - Operation Nickel Grass

During the time of my first deployment, perhaps one of the most outrageous attacks on Israel took place — attacks that left Israel defenseless in the face of the opponents. Although I was not at the forefront of the battle, my small part in the Armageddon-like events left a damping effect on me as a sailor of the US military.

During the 1973 Arab–Israeli War, the United States conducted Operation Nickel Grass, a strategic airlift mission, to provide Israel with supplies and munitions. Between October 14 and November 14 of that year, a number of C-141 Starlifters and C-5 Galaxy aircraft carried about 22,325 tons of supplies, including artillery, ammunition, and tanks, on behalf of the United States Air Force's Military Airlift Command. This operation aimed to strengthen the Israeli military's capabilities against a major combined attack by Egypt and Syria, both heavily backed by the Soviet Union. Even without being on the front lines, the chronology of these events is still etched in my brain.

The Military Airlift Command (MAC) was confronted with an urgent and unanticipated task as the US was withdrawing its massive military presence from Vietnam and preparing to defend Israel during a major conflict. Israel was shocked by a sudden and vicious invasion coordinated by Egypt and Syria on October 6, 1973, during Yom Kippur, a day of great significance and contemplation for the Jewish people. The flimsy truce that had survived the 1967 Arab-Israeli War was destroyed by this raid.

When Israel discovered that it was fighting a bloody war on two fronts, desperation set in. Israel dispatched every commercial aircraft operated by El Al Airline to transport essential military supplies from the United States in a frantic attempt to defend itself. As it became evident that these airlift resources were terribly inadequate for the enormous quantity of supplies, especially the oversized cargo that was required to support its military, the country's fear increased by a lot.

On October 10, when the Soviet Union started airlifting supplies to Egypt and Syria, further tipping the scales against Israel, the anxiety and urgency reached a fever pitch. The circumstances were grave, and there was an urgent and great need for assistance.

After Israeli Prime Minister Golda Meir made a pleading plea, President Richard M. Nixon moved quickly to launch Operation NICKEL GRASS, an airborne resupply mission to Israel, on October 13. The necessity for a flexible and effective military airlift system was highlighted by this operation. En route to Tel Aviv's Lod International Airport, MAC C-141 and C-5 cargo transports continuously brought in desperately needed war equipment from all over the United States for thirty-two anxious and critical days.

The aircraft made a crucial break at Lajes Field in the Azores, which is situated about midway on the arduous 6,450 nautical mile voyage that connects the US and Israel. The world's strong reliance on Arab oil presents a diplomatic minefield, which the C-141 and C-5 planes carefully avoided by staying out of the airspace of neighboring countries. Because of the meticulous preparation, the supplies lifeline reached Israel without escalating geopolitical tensions. Driven by a sense of urgency and resolve, the airlift operation proved the effectiveness of prompt and decisive action during emergency situations.

From the moment the first mission touched down on October 14 to the final landing at Lod on November 14, the Military Airlift Command (MAC) undertook a herculean effort to support Israel in its time of desperate need. Over 567 missions, spanning 18,414 grueling hours of flight, MAC's dedicated crew transported a staggering 22,318 tons of essential supplies. The mighty C-5s, in 145 missions, hauled half of this critical load, while the reliable C-141s, through 422 missions, delivered 10,754 tons. This unusual, urgent, and determined effort gave Israel vital help at one of its lowest points. It was a lifeline. The unrelenting efforts of the aircrews at MAC embodied the spirit of fortitude and unity in the face of difficulty.

But it wasn't just the aircrews that played an important role in the export process. Upon leaving Edinburgh, the carrier and its consorts stood ready to support the airlift operation, preparing to rejoin the Sixth Fleet on October 25, 1973. On October 10th, while docked in Edinburgh, my shipmates and I received urgent orders to mobilize. The Kennedy was to position itself strategically 100 miles west of Gibraltar to support the critical U.S. airlift operation. Our mission was to protect the cargo planes supplying Israel with essential military supplies, including 200 AIM-9 Sidewinder missiles and advanced anti-tank weaponry.

The urgency and gravity of the mission were palpable, casting a sense of determination and resolve among the crew. The Kennedy, a formidable asset in the U.S. Navy, was entrusted with ensuring the safe passage of these vital supplies across the

Mediterranean, a treacherous route fraught with potential threats from hostile forces. The operation demanded precise coordination and unwavering vigilance, with our aircraft flying up to 200 sorties per day to maintain air superiority and provide critical cover for the airlift. Each sortie was a testament to the skill and dedication of our pilots, ensuring the success of a mission of immense geopolitical significance.

By the time the cease-fire was implemented on November 2, the Soviet Union's resupply efforts for Egypt and Syria had been far outpaced by the Military Airlift Command's (MAC) mission in support of Israel. With the help of AN-12 and AN-22 transport planes, the Soviet Air Force completed 935 missions carrying 15,000 tons of supplies.

In contrast, MAC's C-5s and C-141s delivered 22,318 tons of material in 567 missions, a remarkable feat considering the vast distance involved. The enormity of the logistics task was what truly elevated MAC's performance. The average distance traveled by Soviet transports was 1,700 nautical miles, but the American planes traveled 6,450 nautical miles in one direction to reach Israel.

This meant MAC's aircrews not only moved more supplies but did so over distances nearly four times greater, showcasing their extraordinary efficiency and endurance. The accomplishment of this operation demonstrated the competence and commitment of MAC staff members, who surmounted considerable logistical obstacles to guarantee that crucial assistance reached Israel at a crucial juncture.

The remarkable performance of the C-5 aircraft played a significant role in the overwhelming success of Operation NICKEL GRASS. These colossal spacecraft carried an astounding 73 tons on average every flight, a far cry from the C-141's 28 tons. Massive 155mm howitzers, 175mm cannons, M-60 and M-48 battle tanks, Sikorsky CH-53D helicopters, and McDonnell Douglas A-4 Skyhawk aircraft fuselages were all delivered by the C-5 thanks to its exceptional capacity to transport large loads. Such a heavy load was beyond the capability of any other USAF aircraft.

The C-5 saw its first actual combat test during this operation and performed admirably. There was a jolt of hope and resolve when these planes, loaded with essential military equipment, touched down in Israel. The accomplishment of this vital resupply mission was made possible in large part by the commitment and expertise of the pilots, who worked nonstop under extreme pressure. Their actions made a significant difference in Israel's hour of need by demonstrating not just the C-5's extraordinary capabilities but also the unwavering spirit and solidarity in the face of hardship.

The Israeli Airlift highlighted just how vital the U.S. basing facilities at Lajes truly were. It also sparked renewed interest in developing the C-5's aerial refueling capability. If the Portuguese hadn't allowed access to Lajes, and with Germany, Spain, Greece, and Turkey all refusing landing rights, the Military Airlift Command (MAC) would have struggled immensely to carry out Operation NICKEL GRASS. The success of the mission depended heavily on these critical factors, and the operation's challenges emphasized the importance of international cooperation and advanced logistics in times of crisis.

Witnessing these events unfold, I was struck by a mix of awe and anxiety. The realization that the entire operation hinged on a single, fragile thread of international support was both humbling and terrifying. The pressure was immense, knowing that any faltering in the chain could have dire consequences for the mission and the people relying on it. Yet, seeing the cooperation come through, especially from the Portuguese, filled me with a profound sense of relief and gratitude. It was a powerful reminder of how interconnected and dependent we are on each other, especially in moments of global crisis.

On October 6, as Israel came under fierce attack from Egyptian and Syrian forces, a C-5 crew at Patuxent Naval Air Station in Maryland was urgently loading supplies. The atmosphere was tense, charged with the urgency of providing crucial support. The crew was supposed to be flown to Anderson Air Force Base on the island of Guam via the Pacific Ocean as part of the mission.

With the implementation of the cease-fire on January 27, 1973, the Paris Peace Accords formally brought an end to American direct military engagement in Vietnam. The necessity to continue thwarting North Vietnam's aggressive advances into Cambodia, Laos, and South Vietnam, however, overwhelmed whatever relief this accord brought. Anderson AFB's strategic location and mission were vital in this continued struggle.

As the aircraft was prepared for takeoff, the gravity of the mission was clear. The supplies loaded were not just materials but a lifeline, essential for ongoing efforts. The journey ahead was long and demanding, reflecting the critical nature of the task at hand. The significance of Anderson AFB as a hub of support in these challenging times underscored the importance of the mission. The crew united in purpose faced the challenges with determination, knowing that their efforts were a crucial part of a larger operation aimed at providing stability and support in a time of crisis.

From the sidelines, I watched the intense activity. The sight of the massive C-5 being loaded with supplies was both impressive and sobering. The seriousness of the mission was clear as the crew worked with focused determination. I felt a mix of anxiety and admiration, knowing how important this mission was.

As the aircraft prepared for takeoff, I marveled at the operation's scale. The supplies weren't just items; they were essential for the ongoing efforts in Southeast Asia. The long and demanding journey ahead showed the heavy responsibility of everyone involved. Anderson AFB was a crucial support point, and I felt deep respect for the crew's dedication. Their clear purpose and resolve were evident, and I knew their efforts were critical to the mission of providing stability and aid in a time of crisis.

The return journey took the crew through Hickam AFB, Hawaii, arriving back at Dover on October 14. Upon landing, they were met by the squadron's operations officer, who conveyed urgent instructions. The crew was told to wash their flight suits, briefly reunite with their families, and prepare for an immediate mission to Israel.

Less than 36 hours later, they were on the ramp at Wright Patterson AFB, Ohio, loading cargo bound for Tel Aviv. The urgency of the situation was clear, and the importance of each item being loaded was evident. Over the next 17 days, the crew flew four intense missions in support of Operation NICKEL GRASS. Despite the exhaustion, the sense of purpose drove them forward until they reached the maximum allowable flying time, knowing their efforts were making a critical difference.

As with most new technologies, the C-5's advanced navigational systems occasionally encountered issues. Despite having state-of-the-art inertial navigation and Doppler systems for the time, these aids were sometimes prone to failure and were viewed as supplementary tools for navigation. The C-5 was equipped with a full array of navigation equipment, including a sextant, LORAN, and radar. However, due to restrictions on flying over the airspace of Mediterranean border countries, navigating from Lajes through the Mediterranean to Israel often became challenging.

One mission stands out for its particularly tricky navigation. It was dark as the aircraft approached the Straits of Gibraltar, a narrow ten-mile passage between Gibraltar and the Moroccan coast, requiring precise navigation with only five miles of margin on each side of the centerline. Typically, radar would assist in this maneuver, but on this occasion, the radar had failed, and other electronic aids were unreliable. With the aircraft traveling at speeds exceeding Mach 0.78 (530 mph) and flying 5½ miles above the water, the coasts approached quickly, leaving no time for celestial navigation.

The pilot and co-pilot had to rely on visual cues, with the pilot looking out one window and the co-pilot out the other, while the navigator sat in the jump seat between them, visually sighting the ground lights on both coasts. Aided by radio fixes and the support of the U.S. Navy's 6th Fleet, the aircraft successfully navigated the Eastern Mediterranean, where it was met by an Israeli F-4 Phantom escort for a safe approach and landing at Lod Airport.

When considering these events, the aircrews' unwavering resolve and skill came to mind as a ray of hope and resiliency. From the sidelines, it was hard not to be filled with a great deal of admiration for their ability to handle such difficult circumstances with resolute focus and poise. The crucial significance of expertise, collaboration, and global coordination was highlighted by the triumphant fulfillment of their missions.

The sight of the enormous C-5 aircraft served as a potent reminder of human ingenuity and perseverance as it overcame both technical challenges and the complications of international navigation. It was evident that these operations were more than just flights as the Israeli F-4 Phantom escort skillfully guided the C-5 to Lod Airport. They were vital to the larger purpose of offering stability and support during times of crisis.

Ultimately, these courageous crews' efforts demonstrated the incredible extent people will go to in order to assist others, highlighting the significant influence of their commitment and sacrifice. This lasting legacy is a monument to the unwavering courage and dedication of individuals who stand out for what is right in times of need.

Chapter 8: Tangled Web of Diplomacy

The war and its trials and tribulations may have subsided for the time being, but the reality of the situation was such that the threat of imminent devastation was still lingering in the air. We were aboard the USS Kennedy, continuing the tour while Henry Kissinger was occupied with the arduous task of mitigating the situation between the two states.

Kissinger's method involved what became known as shuttle diplomacy. He traveled extensively—between Washington, Tel Aviv, Cairo, and Moscow—working to mediate and de-escalate the conflict. This continuous movement was crucial, representing direct and ongoing efforts to negotiate peace.

For those of us in the military, updates on Kissinger's diplomatic efforts brought us hope. It was comforting to know that the highest authorities were working to end the dispute and stop it from getting worse. His diplomatic strategy was not only about supporting Israel's defense capabilities but also about managing relations with the Soviet Union to avoid an expansion of the conflict.

The ceasefires Kissinger helped to negotiate were critical, though temporary. They did not resolve the conflict entirely, but they were vital first steps toward longer-term peace agreements.

As soon as he assumed office, President Richard Nixon realized that the protracted Arab-Israeli dispute over the seized lands might damage America's reputation in the Arab world and threaten the détente between the US and the USSR. Nixon directed Secretary of State William Rogers to discuss a possible

Middle East solution with the Soviets in an attempt to break the impasse.

The goal was to craft an agreement that both superpowers could present to their respective allies in the region. However, by December 1969, the Soviet Union, Egypt, and Israel had all rejected the so-called "Rogers Plan." This plan proposed that Israel withdraw to its 1949 armistice lines with minor adjustments in exchange for peace.

The failure of the Rogers Plan led Nixon to halt further efforts to negotiate with the Soviets. He increasingly supported National Security Advisor Henry Kissinger's view that the U.S. should avoid pressing Israel for concessions as long as Egypt, the principal Arab state, remained aligned with the Soviets. In the summer of 1970, Nixon overruled Kissinger and allowed Rogers to propose a more limited initiative to end the Israeli-Egyptian "War of Attrition" along the Suez Canal, where Soviet forces were also involved.

This new proposal, known as "Rogers II," called for a three-month ceasefire and negotiations under U.N. mediator Gunnar Jarring. Both Israel and Egypt agreed, and hostilities ceased on August 7. Yet Nixon's enthusiasm for diplomacy was dampened by subsequent Egyptian and Soviet moves to position anti-aircraft missiles closer to the Canal, as well as Syrian involvement in Jordan's civil war. Until February 1971, Kissinger's arguments against prematurely rewarding Soviet allies prevailed.

Egyptian President Anwar Sadat offered a new chance for rapprochement in February 1971. In exchange for the Israeli Defense Forces (IDF) withdrawing from the east bank of the Suez Canal, he suggested that Egypt restore the canal and eventually consented to more withdrawals. Sadat also offered to renounce belligerency against Israel if the IDF pulled back to the international border.

Rogers sought to leverage Sadat's proposal to work toward an interim settlement, but he faced opposition from the Israelis and little support from Kissinger and Nixon. Kissinger doubted that Sadat's interim settlement proposal, along with a Soviet peace plan introduced that September, would be acceptable to the Israelis. He also wanted to avoid any discord over the Middle East that could disrupt the détente efforts before the Moscow summit in May 1972. Nixon, motivated by a desire to maintain stable U.S.-Israeli relations before the 1972 elections, agreed with Kissinger's assessment.

Following the Moscow summit, where the U.S. and the Soviets deliberately avoided discussing the Middle East, Sadat took decisive steps to break the stalemate. In July 1972, he expelled Soviet military advisors from Egypt and established a backchannel to Kissinger through his national security advisor, Hafiz Isma'il. Isma'il spoke with Kissinger in February 1973, letting him know that Egypt was prepared to make a separate peace accord with Israel.

This agreement might have included peacekeepers in sensitive locations like Sharm al-Shaykh and demilitarized zones on both sides of the international boundary. All rehabilitation of ties between Egypt and Israel, Sadat argued, would have to wait until Israel left all of the regions it had conquered in 1967. The Israelis reacted slowly. Neither Nixon nor Kissinger did anything to soften their positions. Sadat expressed his public dissatisfaction and received warnings from Soviet Secretary-General Leonid Brezhnev as well as Jordan's King Hussein.

Nixon and Kissinger, along with a large portion of the U.S. intelligence community, thought Egypt and Syria were unlikely to attack Israel. Nixon and Kissinger made the decision to postpone any further US diplomatic efforts until after Israel's elections in October until the fall of 1973.

Kissinger's diplomatic maneuvers also had to take into consideration the precarious power relations between the United States and the Soviet Union. By strengthening U.S. connections with important regional parties, his policy sought to minimize Soviet dominance in the Middle East and ensure that no single superpower could control the region's geopolitics. This was especially clear in the way he handled the aftermath of the Yom Kippur War in 1973, when he used US assistance to Israel to balance off Soviet backing for Egypt and Syria.

Kissinger was necessary for keeping the balance of power in the Middle East in favor of US interests by stimulating ties with important governments there and reducing Soviet influence.

Kissinger's strategies did not, however, come without consequences. Because they felt like puppets in the bigger game of superpower competition, smaller governments frequently developed hostility toward him due to his dependence on realpolitik and strategic manipulation. This was especially evident in his dealings with the countries of the Middle East, where often immediate diplomatic successes came at the expense of sustained confidence and collaboration.

Furthermore, Kissinger mainly ignored deeper, more structural concerns like Palestinian sovereignty and rights because of his concentration on state-to-state ties. Since basic concerns were ignored, this negligence led to the continuation and even escalation of several regional wars. Thus, by disregarding some of the underlying reasons for instability, Kissinger's policies, although helpful in handling immediate crises, also set the stage for future confrontations.

In contrast, Kissinger's complex balancing acts were not at all like President Ronald Reagan's strategy in the 1980s. Reagan's emphasis on overt demonstrations of American dominance and direct military might reflect a change in U.S. foreign policy toward more overt and conspicuous measures. This was made clear by American operations in Lebanon and Grenada when the main goal was to demonstrate American power rather than participate in the type of complex diplomatic discussions typical of Kissinger's time. Reagan wanted to pacify the area in Lebanon, so he sent Marines there as part of a multinational peacekeeping mission. However, this move eventually demonstrated the limitations of military might in the absence of diplomatic efforts. Reagan also focused on swift military action without thorough diplomatic consultation, justifying the invasion of Grenada as a measure to save American lives and stop Communist growth.

Then there was Roosevelt. With Franklin D. Roosevelt's assistance, the United Nations established a rough plan for international collaboration and to prevent future conflicts through successful diplomacy and collective security measures. Roosevelt had a wide-ranging, utopian vision seeking to achieve stability and peace via collaboration and understanding.

In addition to the desire to back a vital ally, the United States' commitment to Israel was characterized by larger strategic imperatives that were essential to its interests. This strategy involves giving Israel just enough military support to ensure its security and stave off any neighboring invasion but with measures in place to avoid an Israeli victory on the battlefield that could not be clearly declared. The idea was to build up circumstances that would favor a little Israeli win or, better yet, a military impasse that would open the door to negotiations for a solution.

This cautious attitude to military assistance was indicative of a sophisticated comprehension of the Middle East's geopolitical dynamics. By restricting the supplies, the US sought to avoid a major escalation of hostilities that might attract the USSR or cause the war to spiral out of hand. Perennial peace in the area would not be facilitated by either a resounding win or a shattering loss, according to U.S. policy. Rather, the most practical route to a long-term settlement of the conflict was thought to be striking a balance that would benefit Israel just a little while still encouraging both parties to the negotiating table.

In actuality, this meant that although the United States would react to sudden existential threats to Israel, as in the case of the Yom Kippur War, when a large-scale military resupply was judged required, it also involved instances in which Israel was under pressure to curtail its military activities or yield during peace talks. Instead of letting the dispute settle itself by military means alone, which was unlikely to result in a lasting peace, the main objective was to manage the crisis to the point where a diplomatic settlement became attainable.

On October 6, 1973, Israeli forces in the Golan Heights and the Sinai Peninsula came under attack from Egypt and Syria. At first, Israel suffered heavy losses, but Secretary of State and National Security Advisor Henry Kissinger expected an Israeli win quickly. He was worried that Soviet action might follow a decisive Arab defeat, which would strengthen Soviet dominance in the region and damage détente. As a result, Kissinger proposed that the US and the USSR jointly demand a truce and a reversion to the pre-1967 borders. The Soviets, reluctant to directly support their allies, agreed to this proposal, but Egypt declined the ceasefire.

Seeking to prevent an outright Arab defeat without engaging militarily, the Soviets began supplying Egypt and Syria with arms. By October 9, following an unsuccessful Israeli counter-offensive against Egyptian forces, Israel sought American assistance. President Nixon, not wanting Israel to be overrun, agreed to an airlift of military supplies, which began on October 14.

With the American airlift, the tide of the conflict shifted against the Arab states. On the 16th of October, IDF crossed the Suez Canal, and Egypt's leader, Anwar Sadat, began to consider a cease-fire. This led Brezhnev, the commander-in-chief of the USSR, to invite Richard Nixon's National Security Advisor, Kissinger, to Moscow for deliberations. Later on, the United Nations Security Council passed a resolution—UNSC 338 on October 22 which demanded a ceasefire and follow-up with negotiations. Nevertheless, when he visited Tel Aviv, Kissinger suggested through his talk to Israeli leaders that once he was back in Washington, the U. S. would not object to further operations by the IDF. Afterward, Kissinger accepted a Soviet request for another ceasefire resolution, which the Security

Council passed on October 23. Despite this, Israel continued its military operations.

In a menacing letter to Nixon dated October 24, Brezhnev suggested using both Soviet and American forces to uphold the cease-fire. Brezhnev threatened to take unilateral action if the United States refused. In retaliation, the US put its nuclear weapons on worldwide alert on October 25. Later that day, the Security Council's adoption of Resolution 340—which called for a truce, a pullback to October 22 positions, and the deployment of U.N. troops and observers—de-escalated the conflict. Israel consented to the ceasefire this time.

The 1973 war ended with an Israeli triumph, but the US suffered a great deal as a result. The dispute placed the United States and the Soviet Union closer to a nuclear standoff than it had been since the Cuban Missile Crisis, even while détente remained intact. In addition, the U.S. airlift to Israel set off an oil embargo by Arab producers against the United States and a few Western European countries, which caused disturbances to the world economy. This circumstance allowed Kissinger to further his efforts to bring peace between Israel and the Arab world.

Although Kissinger was not the end-all, be-all for the Yom Kippur War, if it wasn't for him, the conflict's mitigation would have been somewhat impossible. Kissinger played a very important role in the adoption of multiple UN Security Council resolutions, including Resolutions 338 and 340. It is evidence of his diplomatic skill in leveraging international institutions to achieve ceasefire agreements. These resolutions were critical in halting hostilities.

Kissinger was not the only player in the Yom Kippur War, but his diplomatic moves were crucial. His capacity for managing superpower relations, strategic vision, and negotiating were essential in defusing the situation and averting a more disastrous escalation. The road to conflict settlement and the ensuing peace initiatives would have been far more difficult without Kissinger's efforts.

Chapter 9: The War's Turning Point

During the conflicts within the Yom Kippur War and the overall Cold War, two regions stood out the most: the Sinai Peninsula and the Golan Heights, making them volatile and prone to conflict as the war grew.

The Arab-Israeli conflict began on October 6, 1973, when Egyptian-Syrian forces, relying on their numerical superiority, launched a coordinated surprise attack on Israeli forces in the Sinai Peninsula and the Golan Heights. At the beginning, the forces on the side that were attacking had some impressive performances.

Egyptian armor and infantry force crossed the Suez Canal and eroded the Israeli-fortified Bar-Lev Line, forcing the latter to retreat. In the same year, Syrian forces overpowered Israeli troops and managed to push Israel back in certain areas of the Golan Heights.

The initial days of the Yom Kippur War saw substantial victories for the Arab forces, causing a serious crisis for the Israeli military, who, under severe pressure and with depleted resources, struggled to contain the offensives. The situation was so dire that Israel found itself in desperate need of international support to continue fighting. The turning point came when the United States decided to intervene.

Despite internal debates, the Nixon administration approved a large-scale airlift of military supplies to Israel, starting on October 10. This decisive support replenished Israeli military stocks, enabling them to regroup and mount a counteroffensive.

By October 9, the tide of the war began to shift. Israeli forces managed to stabilize the front lines, largely because Egypt, having secured its positions in the Sinai, did not press further east to support the Syrians. This allowed Israel to redirect resources to the Golan Heights, where they began to push back the Syrian forces. Once the Syrian threat was mitigated, Israel focused its efforts on the Sinai front, launching successful counterattacks that not only regained lost ground but also captured additional territory from both Egypt and Syria.

The third factor that contributed to the improvement of Somalia's economy was the assistance from the U.S. airlift. With the aid received from American military equipment, Israeli morale and effectiveness were boosted to mount operations. However, this U.S. support came at the cost of creating substantial geopolitical consequences. As a result, the Arab members of the Organization of Petroleum Exporting Countries (OPEC) placed an oil embargo on the U.S., resulting in an energy crisis around the world.

However, the military achievements of the two antagonists were counterbalanced by several incidents that brought the full-scale confrontation within a hair's breadth of dragging in the superpowers. Israel almost continued its operations after a UN ceasefire on October 22. With Egypt and Syria as its allies, the Soviet Union said it would commit troops to stop the Israeli forces from encircling and annihilating the Egyptian Third Army. This forced the United States to increase its military preparedness for Defcon 3, indicating a serious situation with war almost inevitable, similar to the Cuban Missile Crisis. Due to tremendous pressure from the worldwide community, Israel agreed to cease fighting, which helped avoid transforming the situation into a broader conflict.

Thus, the consequences of the Yom Kippur War impacted not only the Middle East but also the global community. The war also ended the stalemate in the peace negotiations that had existed since the end of the 1967 Arab-Israeli war. The urge for military confrontation indicated the inability of military approaches to solve the Arab-Israeli conflict, forcing all sides to look for diplomatic solutions. For Israel, the war brought the realization that there was a need to seek stable peace to avoid falling prey to another unanticipated attack in the future.

The United States, being aware of the financial consequences of the Arab oil embargo and seeing Middle East stability as a vital interest, focused on solving the Arab-Israeli conflict. U.S. Secretary of State Henry Kissinger then initiated what is famously known as shuttle diplomacy, moving from one capital of the involved nations to another in a bid to sell his package for disengagement and ultimate peace in the region. Indeed, while Kissinger did not secure an overall ceasefire and agreement, his efforts led to the signing of several memorable agreements.

When Israel and Egypt signed disengagement agreements in January 1974 and September 1975, they created buffer zones, which significantly minimized the chances of the two sides engaging in war. These agreements were significant in restoring confidence for a lasting peace deal and future negotiations. A similar disengagement agreement was signed by Israel and Syria in May 1974. While it did not culminate in a treaty, it contributed to creating a new status in the Golan region.

The overall premise of the Arab-Israeli conflict and events up to the Yom Kippur War provided the precise preconditions for the Camp David Accords of 1978. Despite these efforts, some important achievements were made through the Carter-facilitated peace agreements, resulting in a peace treaty signed between Israel and Egypt. In this treaty, Israel consented to vacate the Sinai Peninsula, and Egypt, in return, declared recognition and normalization of relations with Israel. This treaty was the first diplomatic agreement in which an Arab country formally recognized Israel and demonstrated that diplomatic solutions could resolve conflicts in this region.

Thus, despite the Yom Kippur War ending large-scale conventional Arab-Israeli wars, it also revealed the challenges of achieving genuine peace in the Middle East. This conflict emphasized the importance of diplomacy and third-party intervention. It also highlighted global relations and the functioning and distribution of power, showing how local wars might lead to world wars.

During the pivotal fights in Sinai and the Golan Heights during the 1973 Yom Kippur War, the USS John F. Kennedy (CV-67) was influential in delivering air support and maintaining air supremacy.

Following a quick three-day visit to Edinburgh, the USS John F. Kennedy's homecoming plans were dramatically changed by a severe situation in the Middle East on October 6, 1973. Egyptian and Syrian soldiers launched a surprise attack on Israel, sparking an immediate military reaction. On October 13, the USS John F. Kennedy sailed from Edinburgh, accompanied by the guided missile frigate Dale (DLG-19), destroyer Richard E. Byrd (DDG-23), and destroyer Sarsfield (DD-837), and assisted by the oiler Caloosahatchee (AO-98). Their target was a strategic holding region located 100 miles west of Gibraltar, chosen to maintain an alert and ready attitude in response to growing Middle Eastern tensions.

This deployment demonstrated the USS John F. Kennedy's critical role as a symbol of American military power and commitment to regional security. As they proceeded into their alert position, the carrier and its escorts prepared to assist prospective military actions, reassure friends, and deter foes. The urgency and intensity of the situation underscored the carrier group's preparedness to respond quickly to any events, emphasizing the interconnectivity of global geopolitics and the crucial role of maritime presence in sustaining international security.

The carrier's deployment to the Eastern Mediterranean was a strategic decision to project US naval force, reassure Israel of American backing, and discourage Soviet action. The carrier's presence acted as a psychological and tactical advantage for Israeli forces, with its aircraft on standby for potential air support missions. Additionally, Kennedy's reconnaissance planes provided vital intelligence on enemy movements and positions, which was crucial for the Israeli Defense Forces in planning and executing their counteroffensives.

The electronic warfare capabilities of the USS John F. Kennedy also contributed to disrupting Egyptian and Syrian communications, thereby enhancing the effectiveness of Israeli operations. The carrier's fighter jets conducted combat air patrols to intercept potential threats from Arab air forces, maintaining air superiority over critical areas. This presence helped prevent enemy aircraft from gaining an advantage and supported the overall air dominance in the region.

A critical component of the carrier's job was to dissuade Soviet intervention. With the Soviet Union offering significant assistance to Egypt and Syria, the presence of the USS John F. Kennedy served as a buffer, keeping the crisis from growing into a direct superpower clash. Furthermore, the carrier offered logistical and operational assistance to allied air forces, such as refueling, resupply, and repair, thus improving the efficacy and sustainability of air missions.

Coordination with the Israeli Air Force meant that air missions were integrated, boosting the effectiveness of air superiority efforts. The deployment of the USS John F. Kennedy reassured US friends in the Middle East of America's commitment to their security, particularly Israel, which faced major threats early in the conflict. The awareness of the US Navy's powerful airpower in the region had a psychological influence on Arab troops and their Soviet allies, causing them to take a more cautious approach to their operations.

The Sinai and Golan conflict, part of the larger Yom Kippur War in 1973, saw several key moments that shifted momentum in favor of Israel. Egypt and Syria staged a surprise strike on Yom Kippur by forming alliances, which triggered the conflict. The Egyptian army crossed the Suez Canal and breached the Bar-Lev Line, allowing them to move into the Sinai Peninsula and have easy access to the area. The Syrian military launched simultaneous strikes on Israeli positions in the Golan Heights.

These early offensives resulted in significant geographical gains for Arab soldiers while claiming many Israeli lives.

In response to these attacks, Israel rapidly mobilized its reserve forces. Despite facing early setbacks, Israeli forces launched counterattacks on both fronts. The Israeli Air Force began to establish air superiority, which supported ground operations and disrupted enemy supply lines. These counterattacks helped to stabilize the situation and prevent further Arab advances.

The Battle of the Chinese Farm was an important turning point in the Sinai campaign. When the Egyptian soldiers aggressively reinforced the region near the Suez Canal, Israeli soldiers, headed by General Ariel Sharon, launched an attack to capture a crossing point across the canal. Despite considerable fatalities, Israeli soldiers successfully established a bridgehead. This allowed Israeli soldiers to infiltrate Egyptian territory, eventually encircling the Egyptian Third Army.

Concurrently with the Battle of the Chinese Farm, Israel launched Operation Gazelle, a counteroffensive across the Suez Canal. Israeli soldiers, led by General Avraham "Bren" Adan, crossed the canal and moved into Egyptian land, forming a salient behind Egyptian lines. This action put Israeli forces in a tactically advantageous position and shifted the balance of power on the southern front.

Israeli soldiers resisted Syria's first assault in the Golan Heights. Key engagements, such as the defense of Nafakh and the Valley of Tears, helped to bring the Syrian onslaught to a halt. Israeli armor and infantry divisions were able to retain their positions and inflict significant casualties on the approaching Syrian forces. After securing the front, Israeli soldiers launched an attack, driving Syrian troops back toward Damascus. This counteroffensive regained lost territory and demonstrated Israel's tactical capabilities.

Throughout the battle, the United States provided critical support to Israel. Operation Nickel Grass, the United States' airlift of military supplies, commenced on October 9. This mission comprised delivering critical weapons, ammunition, and equipment to Israel, which helped to restore its depleting reserves.

The resupply mission meant that Israeli soldiers could continue their operations and retain momentum throughout counteroffensives. U.S. assistance also strengthened Israeli morale and underlined America's commitment to Israel's defense.

As the crisis progressed to a critical point, diplomatic efforts to mediate a truce increased. On October 22, the United Nations Security Council enacted Resolution 338, which called for an immediate cease-fire and the commencement of discussions. The truce was affected by diplomatic pressure from both the United States and the Soviet Union, reflecting the superpowers' wish to avoid further escalations.

By the time the ceasefire went into force, Israeli troops had recaptured much of their lost territory and were in advantageous positions in Sinai and the Golan Heights. The political resolution of the conflict, aided by military achievements, solidified Israel's strategic gains and provided the framework for future peace discussions.

The USS Kennedy may not have seemed like it was just another ship amid massive geopolitical disturbances, but without it, the war would not have proved to be in the favor of the Israeli forces. The lives of the sailors and their determination to maintain constant support were crucial to the expedition in every way, shape, and form.

Chapter 10: The Aftermath of the Battle

During the chaotic 1973 Arab-Israeli War, Arab members of the Organization of Petroleum Exporting Countries (OPEC) took upon a daring feat that shook the world economy. In reaction to the United States' decision to resupply Israel's military, these countries imposed a harsh oil embargo. This act of defiance was more than simply a tactical ploy; it was a strong declaration of political solidarity and resistance. The embargo's influence expanded beyond the United States, hurting other Israel supporters such as the Netherlands, Portugal, and South Africa. It wasn't just about cutting off petroleum shipments to these countries but about exercising new economic strength and shifting geopolitical power equations.

The embargo could not have arrived at a worse moment for the United States, whose economic growth was increasingly dependent on foreign oil. The United States found itself reeling, its economy straining under the weight of fuel shortages and rising costs. For many Americans, the crisis meant waiting in lengthy lines at petrol stations, dealing with unexpected limitations on energy usage, and experiencing a genuine sense of vulnerability. The illusion of a secure future powered by infinite resources was unexpectedly shattered.

President Richard M. Nixon's administration had the arduous job of handling the crisis. The campaign to lift the embargo was more than just a diplomatic problem; it was a test of American fortitude and adaptation. The crisis highlighted a fundamental shift in the global financial landscape, with oil-producing countries exerting their power and altering the parameters of international relations. This marked the beginning of a series of American attempts to address the profound foreign policy challenges born from a deep-seated dependence on foreign oil.

Even before the embargo, OPEC had been challenging international oil corporations' dominance, seeking greater prices and a larger proportion of income for their local subsidiaries. The pressure peaked in April 1973, when the Nixon administration announced a new energy plan to increase domestic oil output. The objective was to lessen the country's vulnerability to external shocks and alleviate rising concerns about fuel shortages.

At the same time, as the conflict unfolded, the conglomerate American consciousness was filled with discontent, worry, and a looming consciousness of the American nation's foiled oil addiction. The loss of 1973 revealed that the United States had no strategy and no energy security, and the subsequent years could be characterized as yielding for the means to prevent the encounter of such a condition.

The imposition of the embargo caused a sudden and severe increase in oil prices, echoing across the world with resounding consequences. As the price of oil per barrel doubled and then quadrupled, consumers were forced to deal with increasing expenditures that stretched household budgets and undermined financial stability. Nations confronted fundamental issues that rattled the very foundations of their economy, and with the dollar's parallel depreciation, the prospect of a worldwide recession loomed enormous.

Stockpiled oil supplies provided some short-term respite in Europe and Japan, but it was a flimsy cushion. The persistent threat of high oil prices and recession sowed discord within the Atlantic Alliance. European nations and Japan found themselves in a painfully awkward position, desperately needing U.S. assistance to secure energy sources yet striving to distance themselves from U.S. Middle East policy, which was seen as a source of their plight.

The United States, facing its own crisis of growing oil consumption and dwindling domestic reserves, became more reliant on imported oil than ever before. The country had to negotiate an end to the embargo amidst harsh domestic economic circumstances, which sapped its international leverage and left its citizens feeling vulnerable and disillusioned. The emotional toll was significant as Americans watched their nation's influence wane and their economic security crumble.

To further complicate matters, the organizers of the embargo made its end contingent on U.S. efforts to broker peace between Israel and its Arab neighbors. This added an emotional and political layer of complexity, making the path to resolution fraught with tension and uncertainty. The world watched anxiously, aware that the outcome would not only shape the geopolitical landscape but also touch the lives of millions, defining a generation's experience with economic hardship and international strife.

Faced with these increasing issues, the Nixon administration took dramatic action on November 7, unveiling Project Independence, a major project aimed at attaining domestic energy self-sufficiency and minimizing America's susceptibility to external shocks. This move was more than a policy choice; it was a beacon of hope for a country plagued by economic instability and growing fear about its future.

Simultaneously, the government launched a vigorous diplomatic effort, presenting its partners with a vision of unity and collective power. They proposed forming a coalition of consumer nations, a united front that would offer strategic depth in these turbulent times. The idea of a consumer cartel controlling oil pricing was also put forth, a plan that promised to wrest some control back from the volatile global market and provide a semblance of stability.

However, these efforts, imbued with hope and determination, met with only partial success. The coalition of consumer nations and the proposed cartel faced numerous challenges, and the results fell short of the ambitious goals. The uneven results mirrored the complexity and limitations of international collaboration, leaving the American public with a bittersweet feeling of accomplishment and lasting vulnerability. This time was distinguished by a mix of cautious optimism and deep-seated dread as the country navigated the dark seas of global economic turmoil, attempting to carve itself a more secure and independent future.

President Nixon and Secretary of State Henry Kissinger faced a challenging task, mindful of the complexity between peace talks to end the conflict and discussions with Arab OPEC members to lift the economic embargo and raise oil production. They knew that, in Arab leaders' views, these concerns were inextricably linked. Driven by the urgency of the situation, the Nixon administration pursued two negotiating paths: one with important oil producers to remove the embargo and another with Egypt, Syria, and Israel to arrange an Israeli departure from the Sinai Peninsula and the Golan Heights.

In November 1973, Kissinger initiated intensive talks with Arab leaders. These discussions were filled with optimism and a heavy load of anticipation. On January 18, 1974, the First Egyptian-Israeli Disengagement Agreement was signed, marking the culmination of these efforts. Although a complete peace agreement remained out of reach, noteworthy progress toward resolving the conflict between Israel and Syria gave a glimmer of hope. This preliminary move toward peace sufficiently persuaded the parties concerned to lift the embargo in March 1974. The easing of the embargo sparked relief and cautious hope, as it represented a key step toward stability in a globe rattled by economic and political uncertainty.

The embargo pointed out a very significant challenge in U.S. Middle East policy: the struggle to balance steadfast support for Israel with the need to maintain close ties with the Arab oil-producing monarchies. The pressure on U.S.-Saudi relations emphasized the emotional and political complexities of this delicate balance. The chaotic events of 1973-1974 highlighted the urgent necessity for the United States to balance its unflinching support for Israel, which is critical to countering Soviet influence in the Arab world, with both its foreign policy goals and domestic economic stability. This time was defined by a strong feeling of urgency and vulnerability as the country negotiated the complex web of diplomatic alliances and financial pressures.

Israel's triumph in the Yom Kippur War was costly in terms of deaths, and many Israelis chastised the government for its lack of preparation. The conflict exposed severe intelligence and strategic shortcomings, causing great public displeasure. This anger peaked in April 1974, when Prime Minister Golda Meir (1898-1978) resigned. Her departure was a watershed moment in Israeli history since it resulted in the nomination of Yitzhak Rabin, who subsequently played a significant role in the Israeli-Palestinian peace talks.

On the Egyptian front, although suffering another military setback at the hands of Israel, Egyptian troops' early achievements considerably improved President Anwar Sadat's standing in the Arab world. These early successes showcased Egypt's military prowess and restored national pride.

Sadat took advantage of this newfound esteem to launch a daring peace initiative. The first of two Egyptian-Israeli disengagement accords agreed upon in 1974 called for Egypt to reclaim areas of the Sinai Peninsula. This step-by-step withdrawal strategy had prepared the foundation for serious peace talks in the coming years.

Camp David Peace Accords refer to the initial peace agreement between the Arab nations and Israel, signed in 1978 by Sadat and then Israeli Prime Minister Menachem Begin. These agreements negotiated by the then US President Jimmy Carter were a success, leading to the signing of the Egypt-Israel Peace Treaties in 1979. This agreement brought a legal end to the two countries' conflict and declared that Israel would pull out of the remaining area in the Sinai Peninsula, which was fully done in the year 1982. The peace pact not only broke the hostility between

Egypt and Israel but also paved the way for future peace negotiations in that region.

Thus, for Syria, the Yom Kippur War is considered detrimental. Initial collaboration with Egypt resulted in some early military victories, but the unexpected Egyptian-Israeli cease-fire left Syria vulnerable. Israel took advantage of this scenario by conquering further land in the Golan Heights.

The war's aftermath significantly undermined Syria's strategic position and morale. In 1979, Syria and other Arab governments agreed to exclude Egypt from the Arab League in response to its peace overtures. This decision underlined the Arab world's significant divides about how to approach Israel, as well as the disparities in national interests and policies across Arab states.

The Yom Kippur War and its lack of aftermath had far-reaching consequences for the Middle East. It changed alliances, triggered important political shifts, and laid the groundwork for future peace negotiations.

The battle also highlighted the complexity of Arab-Israeli relations and the region's delicate balance of power. Despite the terrible toll, the battle eventually prepared the door for a new age of diplomacy and agreements, which continues to shape the Middle East's geopolitical environment.

While American diplomacy often lacked immediate successes, it was pivotal in driving significant advancements in the peace process. The United States seldom spearheaded breakthrough initiatives, yet its active involvement was crucial for progress. Even when U.S. efforts fell short, they frequently catalyzed regional dynamics that eventually bore fruit. For instance,

President Jimmy Carter's early inclination toward a U.S.-Soviet-led initiative spurred Egyptian President Anwar Sadat to take charge, fostering his collaboration with Israeli Prime Minister Menachem Begin and culminating in the Camp David Accords.

Similarly, Secretary of State George Shultz's failed peace plan set the stage for the success of the Madrid Conference. The Camp David summit and Clinton's proposals, though not immediately fruitful, laid the groundwork for peace negotiations in the ensuing years.

The crucial factor is not the brilliance of any specific plan or strategy but the commitment of leaders to pursuing peace. Determined leadership can propel the peace process forward, with the particular path of negotiations being secondary to the dedication to persist, adapt, and overcome opposition. Former U.S. Secretary of State James Baker's diplomacy before the Madrid Conference illustrates this point.

Despite lacking a clear endpoint, Baker's determination to succeed helped navigate the rejectionist stances of both Palestinian and Israeli leaders. This resolute and consistent American leadership offers valuable lessons from the diplomacy that followed the 1973 War.

Reflecting on my engagement in this complex web of diplomacy and peacekeeping elicits a range of emotions. Being a part of this conflict and witnessing resolute leaders' quest for peace has been both humble and enlightening. The complexities and obstacles of each negotiation highlighted the importance of dedication and leadership.

While the voyage was riddled with challenges, the joint efforts to promote peace demonstrated the resilience and hope that can emerge even in the most chaotic times. It has taught me the value of unflinching resolve in the face of adversity, as well as the never-ending effort required to bridge divisions. Ultimately, it has instilled in me a deep respect for the tireless work of those who strive for peace, even when immediate success seems elusive.

Chapter 11: Diplomatic Resolutions

As the war and conflict ensued, the nations decided that it was time for a solution, or at the very least a significant impasse that halted the treacherous turn of events that had been going on in the recent period of time.

The Arab governments were greatly humiliated by Israel's victory in the 1967 Six-Day War. This sparked a strong desire to regain the vast lands they had lost. Egypt and Syria opted for an unwarranted attack during the holy period of Yom Kippur. Now, Yom Kippur is the most sacred day in the Jewish calendar or biblical year as well as in the Jewish week. This makes it apparent that the ambush was intended to be a tad personal. This attack was made on Israeli positions in the Sinai Peninsula and the Golan Heights, catching Israel and the United States off guard.

Prior to this key moment, the Egyptian and Syrian forces had performed countless drills that were widely considered non-threatening by the international world. These movements, however, were only a precursor to a well-planned and catastrophic assault. As violent combat raged, the United States tried to reach a cease-fire deal acceptable to both Israel and the Arab countries.

Initial attempts at a truce were unsuccessful, extending the anguish and uncertainty. The world waited with bated breath as the battle threatened to escalate out of hand. Finally, after a long military stalemate, a breakthrough happened. On October 25, a cease-fire deal with the Soviet Union was achieved after extensive negotiations. This treaty technically ended the conflict, but isolated confrontations occurred in the following months, creating a sense of unresolved tension.

During the 1973 Yom Kippur War crisis, Henry Kissinger stepped into a pivotal role, personally steering the response to the conflict. With focus, he managed all critical meetings, communications, and strategic discussions, backed by intelligence and situation reports from the Operations Center. This was not a collective effort but a concentrated operation helmed by Kissinger, with key support from a trusted few, including Joe Sisco and Brent Scowcroft of the National Security Council.

Kissinger's primary concern was the broader geopolitical stakes. He keenly understood the weight of the Soviet Union's support for Egypt and Syria while the United States stood firmly behind Israel. The thought of Soviet arms prevailing over American arms troubled him deeply. He was resolute that Israel must not fall, driven by both strategic interests and a profound commitment to the security of the Israeli people.

Amid the chaos of war, Kissinger also perceived a glimmer of hope for peace. He saw an opportunity to transform the devastating conflict into a foundation for peace negotiations, recognizing Egyptian President Anwar Sadat's genuine desire for a settlement. This vision drove him to pursue dual objectives: safeguarding Israel from military defeat and ensuring Egypt was not so humiliated that future peace talks would be impossible.

Kissinger's task was a delicate balancing act, fraught with emotional and strategic complexities. He had to protect U.S. interests while nurturing the fragile possibility of lasting peace in a region torn by strife. His efforts were not just about political maneuvering; they were about the lives and futures of millions, making each decision a poignant blend of duty and hope.

This was an extraordinary situation where Henry Kissinger was deeply engaged in frequent exchanges with both the Israelis and Egyptians. He communicated closely with Simcha Dinitz, the Israeli ambassador in Washington and a trusted confidant, ensuring a constant flow of messages to and from the Israeli government. Simultaneously, Kissinger was in regular contact with Cairo, coordinating through Hafiz Ismail, Egypt's national security advisor, a distinguished retired general and diplomat.

The intensity of these communications was remarkable. Messages flowed incessantly between Kissinger and the Egyptian leadership, reflecting the urgency and high stakes of the moment. Every exchange carried the weight of potential outcomes that could shape the future of the Middle East. Kissinger's ability to handle these high-stakes meetings demonstrated his diplomatic skills and emotional endurance. These exchanges were more than simply bureaucratic formalities; they were infused with the ambitions, anxieties, and aspirations of nations on the verge of additional bloodshed or potential peace.

The exchanges during the Yom Kippur War began with a moving statement from the Egyptians. As the crisis escalated, President Sadat contacted the American administration, not with a proclamation of annihilation but with a request for understanding. He made it plain that Egypt's purpose was not to obliterate Israel but rather to restore lost territory. Sadat's statement was full of steely determination and a genuine desire for justice, underlining that Egypt had no intention of invading Israel itself.

During this chaotic moment, the Syrian side maintained a strict communication quiet despite the fact that their simultaneous onslaught constituted a considerable threat. The situation on the Syrian front became increasingly severe for Israel as Syrian troops made a breakthrough that put them perilously near to overrunning Israeli positions on the Golan Heights and threatening the coastal plain. Israel's worry and stress were obvious as it confronted this unexpected and threatening offensive.

On the Egyptian front, Egyptian forces scored a spectacular and unnerving victory in the early stages of the conflict. They crossed the Suez Canal and drove Israeli soldiers back, instilling a feeling of urgency and desperation among the Israeli defenders. In the early days, Israel was caught by surprise, forced to take a defensive attitude, and had to watch as valuable land was abandoned to Egyptian and Syrian assaults. The Israeli troops and residents were shocked and dismayed when they realized they were up against an organized and determined opponent.

The early stages of the battle were loaded with emotional intensity. The Israelis felt a strong sense of vulnerability and a frantic need to regroup and respond. The Egyptians and Syrians were determined to regain their territory and proclaim their rights.

Throughout the battle, Cairo's signals indicated a clear stance: "We have nothing against the US. We hope the United States recognizes that Egypt is only exerting its right to its land. There is no need for Americans in Egypt to be afraid; they will be safe." This feeling was quite different from the heated climate of 1967.

During the war, this line of communication remained open, exploring methods to end the combat and progress peace efforts in accordance with President Sadat's objectives. However, hostilities can gain pace, hampering diplomatic efforts. In the early stages of the fight, Israel was in a dangerous position, attempting to repel the assaults.

As a result, Egypt sought harsh cease-fire terms backed up by Soviet assistance. The US proposed a cease-fire that would restore the pre-conflict lines, implying that Egyptian forces would withdraw across the Suez Canal. Understandably, Egypt refused to accept these criteria, obstructing the route to peace.

Throughout the occurrence of these events, the USS John F. Kennedy was consistently on standby, ready to support the troops if they needed it.

As the conflict progressed, the Israelis stabilized their front lines and began reclaiming lost territories on both the Syrian and Egyptian fronts. Israel's core borders were never threatened; the primary threats targeted Israeli forces in Sinai and the Golan Heights.

The Israelis initially faced significant challenges, including heavy aircraft losses. Lacking a preemptive strike, they couldn't disable the Egyptian Air Force on the ground as in 1967. The Egyptians' fortified anti-aircraft defenses, including shoulder-held SAM-2 missiles, were highly effective.

Concerned about their dwindling reserves, the Israelis requested an airlift of supplies from the U.S. while the Egyptians turned to the Soviets. Both superpowers began resupplying their allies, each accusing the other of prolonging the war.

Henry Kissinger emphasized supporting the Israelis militarily while stabilizing the situation to prevent a total defeat for Egyptian President Sadat. The Israelis reclaimed the Golan Heights from the Syrians and pushed them back, threatening Damascus. On the Egyptian front, General Ariel Sharon's maneuver placed Israeli units back across the Suez Canal into Egyptian territory.

The war reached a critical point, with both sides suffering significant losses. The Egyptians lost their initial advantage, and the Syrians were nearly defeated. A military stalemate formed, prompting Soviet Premier Leonid Brezhnev to propose a joint U.S.-Soviet ceasefire. Concerned about another Egyptian defeat, Brezhnev urged Nixon to send Kissinger to Moscow.

Kissinger organized a team and flew to Moscow. Despite their fatigue, they met with Brezhnev for preliminary talks, delaying immediate negotiations. The following day, they agreed on ceasefire terms, which were communicated to the involved parties and presented as a joint U.S.-Soviet resolution in New York, effectively ending the conflict.

The Israeli forces did not halt their military operations at the agreed-upon time, leading to a rapidly evolving situation. As a result, they continued their westward advance beyond the Canal even after the ceasefire was implemented on October 22. Initially, it appeared they were heading toward Cairo, but they redirected southwards to the city of Suez, encircling and isolating the Egyptian Third Army, cutting off their supply lines, including essential food and medical supplies.

This created a precarious situation, with accusations that the Israelis had taken advantage of the ceasefire. In desperation, Sadat called for U.S. and Soviet intervention to stop the Israelis and save the Third Army. The Soviets agreed to respond, prompting Kissinger to put U.S. forces on alert to counter any Soviet moves, thus averting a potential crisis when Sadat withdrew his request. Both superpowers then agreed to push for a U.N. resolution to introduce peacekeeping forces.

The Egyptians and Soviets demanded that the Israelis retreat to their positions as of October 22. While fighting had ceased on the Canal's east side, the situation remained tense, with forces still in place. The Syrian front was at a stalemate, with Israeli forces in close range of Damascus.

Kissinger saw an opportunity to negotiate a broader resolution. The immediate concern was resupplying the encircled Egyptian Third Army. Initial talks in Washington with Egyptian Foreign Minister Ismail Fahmy and the Israelis led to Kissinger's trip to the Middle East to meet Sadat directly.

Kissinger's trip included stops in Morocco and Tunisia to garner support before arriving in Cairo on November 6, 1973. Sadat orchestrated a dramatic private meeting with Kissinger at his war headquarters, leaving their delegations to wait outside. This extended discussion led to an agreement on principles to relieve the Third Army and initiate broader negotiations for disengaging forces.

The plan involved allowing essential supplies, excluding arms, through Israeli lines to the Egyptian Third Army, monitored by U.N. troops from Cyprus. Despite initial mistrust, the arrangement was finalized. Key figures like Hal Saunders and Joe Sisco were sent to Israel to secure its government's agreement, while the rest of the delegation proceeded to Jordan and Saudi Arabia. This complex negotiation marked a significant step toward stabilizing the region.

Regardless, on October 22, 1973, the Security Council enacted United Nations Resolution 338, which was a vital action aimed at bringing the Yom Kippur War to an end. During this fight, Israel defended itself against Egypt and Syria's coordinated strikes. The resolution, which was brief and unclear in wording, passed unanimously with one abstention. It urged an immediate ceasefire that would last 12 hours and the full execution of UN Resolution 242 (1967), which detailed criteria for a peaceful settlement in the Middle East. Furthermore, Resolution 338 called for the start of discussions under suitable auspices to build a permanent and enduring peace.

Egypt and Israel initially approved the resolution the same day it was enacted. Syria, under pressure from the Soviet Union, did not accept until the next day. Despite the resolution's adoption, hostilities persisted, highlighting the difficulties in executing such international mandates. In reaction to the continuous conflict, the Security Council passed additional sanctions, UN Resolutions 339 and 340, on October 23 and 25, respectively. These successive resolutions reaffirmed the need for an end to the war and the basic objectives of Resolution 338.

The acceptance of these resolutions was critical to gradually decreasing the intensity of the war. Although the battle lasted for some time, continuous international pressure and diplomatic efforts finally resulted in the halt of hostilities, signaling the conclusion of the Yom Kippur War. This sequence of resolutions illustrated the intricate interplay between diplomacy, international pressure, and the reality of wartime talks in establishing peace.

While these events played out, the USS Kennedy was a member of the Sixth Fleet, which was responsible for maintaining a strong American naval presence in the Mediterranean. The major goal was to give assistance to US allies and avoid further escalation of the war. The carrier's air wing, which included a mix of fighter planes and surveillance aircraft, performed constant patrols to monitor the situation and assure the safety of US interests and partners in the region.

The USS Kennedy's presence also demonstrated American military strength and determination. It delivered a strong message to both the Soviet Union, which was supporting Egypt and Syria, and the combatant states themselves, indicating that the US was highly engaged in the outcome of the battle. This display of power was designed to keep the war from spreading outside the region and to deter direct Soviet action.

Chapter 12: The Return Home

Finally, things were starting to calm down on board the USS John F. Kennedy. A precarious ceasefire was in effect when the Yom Kippur War came to an end. We were nearing the end of our assignment, which had grown far beyond its initial scope. As the crew got ready to return to the US, there was a noticeable sense of relief.

The eagerly anticipated orders to head back home finally arrived on November 14, 1973. The idea of being with our family again energized us after months of intensive procedures. I was struck with a mixture of feelings as we left the Mediterranean: relief, exhaustion, and a deep sense of accomplishment.

As we sailed home, we were left to process our thoughts and feelings in solitude. It was taking us some time to process the full scope of our engagement in the conflict, and it was challenging to reconcile our experiences with the world we were going back to. Every seaman handled things differently; some took comfort in their fellow sailors, while others turned within, struggling under the weight of what they had seen and done. The journey home was not just a physical return but an emotional and mental reckoning with the silent burdens we carried.

Despite the challenging weather and choppy sea, we managed to maintain a positive attitude. We were now stronger because we had confronted the unknowns of battle. Every day took us one step closer to home, and the friendships my shipmates and I had formed during the battle bore witness to that.

The excitement mounted as we got closer to the US East Coast. After being gone since April 1973, we were quite happy about the prospect of celebrating Christmas with our loved ones. The sight of the coast of the United States was a comfort. We felt a deep sense of satisfaction and closure when we eventually docked at Mayport, Florida, on December 1, 1973.

The days that followed were filled with heartfelt reunions and intimate celebrations. Steve, Philip, and I cherished the time with our families. Each embrace and shared smile was like a balm for the months of separation and uncertainty. We recounted our experiences, the stories of our mission mingling with the emotions we had kept at bay.

Reflecting on the impact of the Yom Kippur War, we felt a mix of pride and sorrow, knowing the gravity of what we had endured. The return to normalcy was a stark contrast to the intensity of our mission, but it was a welcome change, grounding us in the simple joys of home and the comforting presence of loved ones. In the 1970s, communication with home was limited to letters, a far cry from the instant connectivity of today. Waiting weeks for a response added to the sense of isolation. Many of us had poured our thoughts and fears onto paper, only to be met with delayed or muted reactions, as if our struggles existed in a separate reality.

Hence, each moment spent with family was a reminder of what we had fought for and a step toward healing from the silent burdens we carried.

However, our return was not greeted with heroism by the masses that existed in the nation since the war was kept secret from most people. Unaware of the conflict we had been embroiled in, friends and family welcomed us with the same informal friendliness that follows any extended absence. Even those closest to us were unaware of a great deal of what we had gone through.

To add fuel to the fire, most of us were still processing our thoughts and feelings and didn't know the breadth of our involvement. The gravity of our roles and the potential consequences of our actions weighed heavily on us, yet we continued with our duties, often without fully comprehending the larger picture. This sense of ambiguity and uncertainty left us grappling with our conscience and the implications of our work.

I struggled with my involvement with nuclear weapons. As a weapons specialist, I was responsible for the weapons loading team that verified and loaded the nuclear weapons on the aircraft. The meticulous nature of this task required not only technical precision but also an unwavering focus. Each step in the process was critical; a single mistake could have catastrophic consequences. The responsibility of ensuring that these weapons were correctly loaded and secured was a burden that often kept me awake at night. The thought that I played a direct role in potentially unleashing such destructive power was a constant source of inner conflict. It was a paradox of duty and ethics, where the line between service and moral responsibility blurred, leaving me questioning the true impact of my actions.

The shift from the chaos of the battlefield to the calm of home was difficult. Memories of the battle would frequently emerge, filling me with feelings of fear, despair, and worry. The quick transition from a high-stress environment to the calm of home life was disconcerting. It left me feeling out of place and alienated from the world around me.

However, I found solace in my family's support and the bonds I formed with my shipmates. My family was an endless supply of love and compassion, guiding me through the difficult emotions of my return. Their presence comforted me and made me realize that I was not alone on this trip. My bond with my shipmates was equally important. We confronted the reintegration obstacles together, drawing strength from our shared experiences. The bonds we formed during our military carried over into our civilian life, forming a support network that was critical in assisting us in adjusting. We faced the challenges of reintegration together, drawing on the determination and solidarity that had sustained us during the war.

Looking back on those days, I feel a strong feeling of pride. We served our nation and contributed to a significant historical event. Coming home was a mixture of relief and nostalgia as we left behind the hardships of war and returned to the familiar comforts of home. Each step closer provided a sense of success and thankfulness for the sacrifices we had made.

The strength of the human spirit was clear in our shared experiences and the bond we had formed. The support we gave and received from each other showed how strong unity can be. Our determination helped us get through the challenges we faced, both in battle and on our return. These moments highlighted the importance of sticking together during tough times.

The emotional trip was difficult. As the memories of combat faded, I developed a strong appreciation for the ordinary pleasures of everyday life. I found myself appreciating tiny moments like a peaceful evening with family or the tranquility of a morning sunrise. These were the things I had struggled to keep, and they meant much more to me now.

Reconnecting with loved ones was both joyful and a little bittersweet. There was an unspoken understanding among us veterans, a shared sense of what we had gone through. Our conversations were a mix of laughter and serious reflection as we processed our experiences together. The brotherhood and mutual respect we had built in the field continued to be a source of strength and comfort.

Coming home was more than a physical return. For me, it was also an emotional and mental one. It was a time for healing, reconnecting, and discovering a new normal. Throughout it all, the force of togetherness and support showed brilliantly, helping us through the shift and reminding us of our collective resilience.

Chapter 13: Personal Reflections

The Yom Kippur War was not just a series of battles; rather, it was a tremendously moving event that will always be carved in my memory. I was struck by the conflict's intricacy and the lessons it taught when I thought back on those hard weeks. The conflict was a sobering reminder of how brittle peace is and how vital alertness and readiness are.

The actual worth of responsibility and sacrifice was among the most important things I ever learned. I had always understood the value of service as a U.S. Navy sailor, but the war expanded my perspective in ways I could not have predicted. Our strong sense of duty to our nation, our allies, and one another developed into a steadfast force that directed all of our decisions. We were a part of something far bigger than ourselves; we weren't just individuals. Our relationships were established beyond space and time by our companionship, shared struggles, and united resolve. Not only were our combined efforts significant, but they also changed lives and left a lasting impression on our hearts and spirits.

The relationships I developed with my shipmates, particularly Steve and Philip, were another incredibly poignant part of the journey. Our solidarity turned into our strength when faced with hardship. Through the hardest times, we confided in one another and shared times of dread, hope, and unwavering resolve. These bonds, which were forged in the furnace of struggle, went beyond simple companionship and turned into lifelines. Long after the war was over, the close bond we forged during those terrifying days persisted, making an enduring impression on our hearts and influencing who we are today.

I now have a deeper understanding of diplomacy's complexity because it had a crucial role in how the Yom Kippur War turned out. Henry Kissinger and other diplomats' ceaseless efforts were not just calculated maneuvers but also lifelines that helped broker ceasefires and prevent a more extensive and possibly disastrous war. It was nothing less than a master class in strategic negotiation to manage the tightrope of backing Israel without coming into open conflict with the Soviet Union. It was enlightening and humbling to observe these diplomatic moves firsthand. It highlighted the enormous influence of discussion and compromise, exposing the importance and vulnerability of peace initiatives.

The battle also made clear how vital foreign alliances and steadfast backing are. During Operation Nickel Grass, the US airlift served as a potent example of the resilience of the US-Israeli relationship. The operation's enormous scope and logistical difficulties were intimidating, but they also demonstrated the US's unwavering commitment to its friends. This support was a powerful declaration of respect and unity that went beyond just military assistance. It demonstrated the strong ties that bind nations together in the face of shared ideals and objectives. The operation served as more than simply a calculated move; it was a moral lifeline, a ray of hope, and a confirmation of our faith in the strength of our combined strength.

The Yom Kippur War was not kept a secret. Both during and after the events, the confrontation was extensively covered in the media. Nonetheless, details of the conflict and the ensuing political gamesmanship were withheld.

Military strategies, movements, and specifics of certain operations were often kept confidential to maintain the element of surprise and protect soldiers' lives. The involvement of external powers, particularly the United States and the Soviet Union, was carefully managed to avoid escalating Cold War tensions. Diplomatic efforts and backchannel communications were frequently conducted in secret to broker ceasefires and negotiate peace without public pressure.

Both Israel and the Arab states involved had reasons to control the narrative within their countries. For Israel, managing public morale and preventing panic was crucial, while Arab states like Egypt and Syria needed to maintain support for their governments and military actions. Revealing too much about the extent of foreign support, especially from the U.S. to Israel and from the Soviet Union to the Arab states, could have complicated international relations. The U.S., for example, wanted to avoid openly flaunting its extensive logistical support to Israel (Operation Nickel Grass) to prevent further strain on its relations with Arab nations.

The United States aimed to position itself as a neutral broker for peace. Highlighting its direct military support for Israel could have hindered its ability to negotiate peace agreements and maintain diplomatic balance in the Middle East. Thus, while the war itself was not secret, certain details and strategic elements were kept confidential to effectively manage military, diplomatic, and domestic challenges.

The 1973 Arab-Israeli War saw immense efforts from military personnel, particularly those involved in critical operations like Operation Nickel Grass. But, the sailors in the Navy and other service members who carried out these missions flawlessly were not acknowledged by the public when they returned. Their contributions were not honored with ceremonies, and their bravery and devotion were not recognized with awards.

The delicate nature of the operations and the larger geopolitical backdrop played a major role in the lack of public recognition. In addition to trying to establish itself as a neutral mediator for any future peace accords between Israel and its neighbors, the United States also wanted to manage the diplomatic ramifications of its active engagement in the conflict. Demonstrating the vast military assistance given to Israel, which included the crucial airlift operation, may have caused tensions in U.S. relations with Arab countries and hindered efforts to mediate peace in the area.

The U.S. administration gave long-term strategic aims precedence over immediate recognition of individual and unit accomplishments by withholding the specifics of these operations and abstaining from public celebrations. Even at the risk of losing public recognition, the sailors and other military personnel recognized the significance of their mission and the need to maintain operational secrets.

Thinking about the wider effects of conflict, I am reminded of the historical influence on modern geopolitics. The Yom Kippur War significantly altered regional dynamics, military tactics, and diplomatic ties in the Middle East. The decades-long resonance of that crucial moment serves as a sobering reminder of the continuous pursuit of peace and stability in the area. The lessons that conflict taught us highlight how complicated international relations are and how important it is to always be alert, prepared, and diplomatic.

Because not fifty years later, there was an attack made by Hamas on Israel. Hamas launched an attack on Israel in October 2023 because of a confluence of social, political, and historical elements. Many nations have classified the Palestinian militant group Hamas as a terrorist organization. Hamas has long-standing grievances against Israel. These complaints have their origins in the larger Israeli-Palestinian conflict, which includes disagreements over sovereignty, land, and the Palestinian refugees' right of return. In the Palestinian territories, Hamas frequently tries to establish its authority and supremacy, especially in Gaza, where it has a stronghold. One could argue that attacking Israel is a means of mobilizing support and proving one's dedication to the Palestinian cause.

It is noteworthy that the strike occurred on the 50th anniversary of the Yom Kippur War. Militant organizations occasionally pick important dates in an effort to invoke memories of previous battles and struggles, to send a message, or to draw historical analogies. There is still no resolution to the Israeli-Palestinian issue, and the violence has periodically escalated.

It is complicated and dependent on a number of variables whether the United States can stop a wider war in the Middle East. Even though it possesses a lot of power, the United States' ability to avoid conflict is dependent on a number of important factors. To engage with all parties concerned and promote communication and talks, the United States can use its diplomatic channels. Making the most of these connections can assist in forming a coalition that seeks to uphold peace and avoid violence.

The United States can also influence regional actors' conduct through economic incentives and punishments. The United States can incentivize nations to seek peaceful solutions instead of waging war by providing financial assistance or levying financial penalties. In order to prevent aggression, the United States has its armed forces stationed in the Middle East.

To deter hostile measures, the United States can show that it is prepared to defend its interests and friends. It is imperative that the threat posed by terrorist groups—which frequently intensify regional conflicts—be addressed. In order to break up terrorist networks and stop them from growing stronger, the United States can carry on collaborating with regional administrations. Working together with powerful nations and international organizations like the United Nations can aid in coordinating.

But, a number of obstacles may prevent these initiatives. The United States' attempts to mediate peace are hampered by long-standing rivalries, notably those between Saudi Arabia and Iran. Achieving long-lasting solutions might be challenging due to the volatile and unpredictable nature of Middle Eastern domestic politics. There are other superpowers, like China and Russia, that have their own interests in the Middle East that can clash with US goals. Even with diplomatic attempts, hostilities might resurface due to unsolved concerns and long-standing historical grievances.

Hence, while the U.S. has the tools and influence to help prevent a wider war in the Middle East, success depends on a nuanced and multi-faceted approach that addresses both immediate tensions and underlying causes of conflict. The outcome is not guaranteed and requires sustained and coordinated efforts.

Thinking about the wider effects of conflict, I am reminded of the historical influence on modern geopolitics. The Yom Kippur War altered regional dynamics, military tactics, and diplomatic ties throughout the Middle East. It was a watershed moment that has had a lasting impact over the years, serving as a reminder of the continuous struggle for regional peace and security.

The significance of the war in my life cannot be emphasized. It solidified my determination, expanded my feeling of responsibility, and molded my outlook on the world. From the experience, I gained an understanding of the importance of flexibility and perseverance in the face of difficulty. It also reinforced my beliefs about the need to remain true to one's principles and the power of unity.

I frequently found myself thinking back on the battle and its timeless lessons in the years that followed. The tough weeks I spent there lingered vividly in my memory, serving as a daily reminder of the enormous stakes of international conflicts. The fight put my skills to the test and forced me to go above and beyond. It was more than just a struggle to survive; it was a furnace that gave me a deep sense of fulfillment and purpose.

There are physical and invisible wounds from the conflict. I can still feel the weight of the choices I made, the loss I suffered, and the echoes of the battlefield. Nevertheless, in the midst of the mayhem and destruction, I found a resilience I had no idea I had.

I am incredibly appreciative of my shipmates' friendship, my family's constant support, and the significant opportunities I had to serve my nation as I reflect back on my voyage. My life was drastically altered by the Yom Kippur War, which left an enduring mark on the fundamental fabric of who I am.

The constant backing of my family gave me the fortitude to face my worst moments. Their love-filled and hopeful letters were like lifelines, keeping my spirits uplifted. My friendship with my shipmates was created in the furnace of combat and grew to be a fraternity that went beyond the lines of battle. We faced the unthinkable together, leaning on one other for bravery when we were scared and hopeless.

Returning from the war meant not just resuming routine but also entering a new stage of life. It was a time for healing, processing the events, and getting back in touch with the people and places that really meant something. Although the conflict had left its imprint, it also made me more determined and increased my awareness of how valuable peace is.

I carry the lessons learned during the Yom Kippur War with me as I go. They act as a mentor, instilling in me the value of responsibility, selflessness, and perseverance. Although the conflict is now in the past, its effects are still felt on my life's journey. It is evidence of the enduring influence of life and the significant ways in which it molds the people we become.

Chapter 14: The Legacy of the Yom Kippur War

No matter how small, war always leaves a residue behind in the region where the conflict occurs. Apart from the lives that are lost, certain political and geographical shifts always come about. Many nations have suffered internal wars and outsider interventions, resulting in damaged state institutions and persistent instability. The long-term impacts of conflict on Middle Eastern geopolitics have been significant and diverse, changing the area in a variety of ways throughout the years.

This fragmentation has made it impossible for certain countries to sustain coherent governments, resulting in prolonged turmoil and power vacuums that are frequently filled by non-state actors. For example, the collapse of central authority in Iraq and Syria has resulted in the formation of formidable militia groups and terrorist organizations that question these countries' legitimacy and sovereignty.

War has intensified sectarian differences, widening the gap between various religious and ethnic groupings. These differences have been both a cause and a result of conflict, perpetuating cycles of violence and distrust. The politicization of sectarian identities has emerged as a defining aspect of Middle Eastern politics, shaping regional alliances and rivalries. In Iraq, Lebanon, and Yemen, sectarianism has caused political gridlock and hampered efforts to develop inclusive and efficient administration.

As conflicts have heightened geopolitical rivalry among regional powers, nations such as Iran, Saudi Arabia, and Turkey have competed for influence, frequently backing opposing forces in combat zones to promote their strategic goals. These conflicts have molded regional alliances and spawned proxy wars, hindering attempts for peace and security. The fight for regional domination has also led to long-running conflicts, as seen in Syria and Yemen, where external parties continue to play important roles.

The humanitarian cost of war has been enormous, with millions of people displaced, infrastructure damaged, and economies ravaged. The long-term social and economic consequences of conflict have stifled progress and worsened poverty and unemployment. The displacement issue has also had geopolitical ramifications, impacting neighboring nations and regions outside the Middle East. Jordan, Lebanon, and Turkey have been hit most by refugee influxes, putting a strain on their resources and changing their demographics.

Foreign countries' engagement in Middle Eastern wars has had long-term consequences for the region's geopolitics. External interventions, whether through direct military action or indirect assistance from local proxies, have frequently resulted in protracted wars and convoluted settlement procedures. Foreign military outposts, as well as the influence of global powers, continue to alter the Middle East's strategic environment. The United States, Russia, and other foreign entities have all played important roles in determining combat outcomes and regional power dynamics.

War has affected economic operations, such as oil production and commerce, which are critical to the economy of many Middle Eastern countries. Infrastructure devastation and the need for lengthy repair have burdened national budgets and redirected resources away from economic programs. Furthermore, the instability in oil prices driven by fighting has had a worldwide economic impact. The region's economic volatility has also had an impact on global energy costs, contributing to economic anxiety in other regions of the world.

Non-state entities, such as terrorist organizations and militias, have gained power and influence as a result of war-related instability. These organizations have used the instability to seize control of territory, challenge official authority, and undertake activities both within and outside the region. Their presence has added another degree of complication to the Middle East's geopolitical landscape. Groups such as ISIS and Hezbollah have emerged as key participants in regional politics and security.

Long-term battles have caused adjustments in alliances and diplomatic ties. Countries have refocused their foreign strategies on fresh dangers and possibilities, sometimes forming unexpected alliances. Diplomatic attempts to settle disputes have also developed, with regional and international entities taking on critical responsibilities in mediation and peacebuilding. The rehabilitation of relations between Israel and numerous Arab nations, mediated by the Abraham Accords, exemplifies how shifting alliances are transforming the area.

The continuous state of violence has had major cultural and sociological consequences, impacting the collective psyche of communities. War has created a culture of resilience but also of pain and loss. These events established national identities and cultural conventions, influencing how communities see themselves and their role in the world. War-related cultural transformations affected everything from art and literature to political discourse and social movements.

The long-term aftermath of the war within the Middle East has been the major factor defining modern US foreign policy and military strategy. The involvement of the USA in the region can be traced back several decades ago when its policies and actions were stipulated by the changing geopolitical situation. The most prominent outcome is steps toward a foreign policy powerfully oriented toward counterterrorism. The growth of organizations like Al-Qaeda and ISIS caused the United States to put its focus on combating terrorism through not only direct military engagement but also by assisting local troops. This concentration has motivated multiple military actions, including the invasions of Afghanistan and Iraq, as well as continuous drone attacks and special operations missions throughout the region.

The United States maintains bases positioned in Qatar, Bahrain, and Kuwait. This presence is designed to project power, safeguard critical interests such as oil pipelines, and offer fast reactions. The necessity to confront regional threats and preserve stability has justified the ongoing development of these sites and the deployment of thousands of US soldiers. To offset the impact of adversaries like Iran, the United States has built strategic ties with major regional states such as Saudi Arabia, Israel, and Egypt.

Given that the Middle East is one of the major oil-producing areas in the globe, energy security has always been the basis of

US foreign policy. As a consequence of guaranteeing the safety of oil supplies and the unhindered passage of energy resources over crucial barriers like the Strait of Hormuz, US participation in the area has grown. The United States has made significant investments in protecting these interests, both via military presence and diplomatic attempts to stabilize the region. However, the United States' participation in the Middle East has not been without obstacles and complaints.

The military operations in Afghanistan and Iraq have generated controversy due to disagreements over their costs and efficacy. There have been requests to review US military commitments and look into alternate methods of accomplishing strategic goals because of the financial and human costs.

A more international approach to Middle Eastern geopolitics has been adopted in recent years. The United States has made a greater effort to collaborate with foreign organizations and partners to solve regional issues. This strategy involves supporting UN peacekeeping operations, promoting regional cooperation through programs like the Gulf Cooperation Council, and engaging in diplomatic attempts to resolve disputes. In light of shifting geopolitical conditions, U.S. foreign policy and military doctrine in the Middle East are expected to continue altering in the future. While continuing efforts to combat terrorism and guarantee energy security, the emphasis may move toward confronting new challenges like cyberwarfare and climate change.

Experts in both history and military affairs have offered comprehensive evaluations of the Yom Kippur War, each contributing their distinct viewpoints to the intricate affairs of the fight. Abraham Rabinovich, a historian best known for his in-depth narrative "The Yom Kippur War: The Epic Encounter That Transformed the Middle East," places special emphasis on the psychological issues and intelligence shortcomings that contributed to Israel's early lack of readiness. He asserts that the Israeli military officials ignored apparent indications of the impending attack because they were blinded by an arrogant sense of self-respect and superiority.

Elinor Burkett denies conventional knowledge by stating that Golda Meir was the key figure of the Yom Kippur War and portrays her as a strong leader who helped Israel recover and win the war. According to Burkett, persistence and critical strategic decisions for changing the course of the fight characterized Meir's leadership during the war, contrary to conventional knowledge.

Despite her initial unpreparedness and the overwhelming surprise attack by Egyptian and Syrian forces, Meir's response was instrumental in maintaining Israeli morale and strategic coherence. At the war's critical juncture, when Defense Minister Moshe Dayan was contemplating surrender and the possibility of a catastrophic defeat, Meir made the bold decision to ready Israel's nuclear arsenal. This doomsday scenario emphasized her determination to ensure the nation's survival at all costs, highlighting her willingness to take extreme measures if necessary.

Historian Walter Laqueur, in his book "The Road to War: The Origins and Aftermath of the Arab-Israeli Conflict 1967-1973," discusses the critical role of U.S. support for Israel. He emphasizes how the U.S. saw Israel as a crucial ally in the Middle

East, a region of significant strategic importance due to its oil reserves. The U.S. airlift of military supplies to Israel, known as Operation Nickel Grass, was a turning point in the conflict. This operation ensured that Israel had the necessary resources to counter the initial successes of the Egyptian and Syrian forces.

Laqueur highlights that this support was not just about aiding an ally but also about demonstrating the futility of Soviet-supported Arab militarism. This action helped the U.S. maintain its influence in the Middle East and counter Soviet expansion. Secretary of State Henry Kissinger played a pivotal role in managing the U.S. response, balancing military support with diplomatic efforts to eventually broker a ceasefire.

The 1973 War of Yom Kippur and the still-ongoing fight in 2024 between Israel and Hamas drastically differ in background, scope, and global consequences. The Yom Kippur War began with a surprise invasion by Egypt and Syria on Yom Kippur to regain land lost in 1967.

It involved comprehensive conventional warfare with two major tank battles on the Sinai Peninsula and Golan Heights. Israel's early unpreparedness was caused by intelligence blunders and overconfidence. Despite this, Prime Minister Golda Meir's bold initiatives, such as fast mobilization and obtaining a US airlift of military supplies, proved critical in reversing the tide. The battle triggered a global energy crisis because of an Arab oil embargo, which culminated in the Camp David Accords, which substantially impacted Middle Eastern geopolitics.

In contrast, the current 2024 Israel-Hamas battle began with Hamas' organized assault from Gaza, which included land, sea, and airstrikes. This fight is marked by asymmetrical urban warfare, heavy civilian deaths, and Hamas' widespread use of subterranean tunnels. Israel's reaction has included airstrikes and ground operations in heavily populated urban areas, causing massive devastation in Gaza. This conflict is exacerbated by regional circumstances, like conflicts with Hezbollah in Lebanon and widespread Iranian backing for Hamas. The continued bloodshed undermines prospective peace discussions, like those with Israel and Saudi Arabia, and contributes to regional instability.

The Yom Kippur War had enormous Cold War consequences, with the United States and the Soviet Union both heavily participating and backing their respective allies. It highlighted the strategic importance of the Middle East and prompted a rethinking of military and intelligence policies. The present fight, which has large international ramifications, demonstrates the changing character of warfare in the area, from state-centered battles to asymmetrical warfare, including non-state players. The larger complications include effects on US foreign policy, regional relationships, and the Middle East's general stability. Both battles highlight the region's persistent complexity and volatility, with each changing the geopolitical environment in dramatic ways.

But if there is one thing that both these wars have in common, it is the destruction that occurred and the lives that were lost. Both sides suffered heavy fatalities during the Yom Kippur War, with thousands of troops and civilians dead or wounded. The ongoing fight with Hamas has also resulted in significant loss of life and severe devastation, especially in heavily populated metropolitan areas.

These conflicts have had an unimaginable human cost, tearing apart countless families and destroying whole towns. The physical infrastructure, which had been meticulously created over the years, is reduced to rubble in a matter of days, creating a landscape of devastation and misery. The environmental effect is also significant, with bombings leaving scars on landscapes and depleting natural resources. As we consider the future, we remain hopeful that the cycle of violence may be ended by understanding, discussion, and a commitment to peace. The idea of a future in which peace triumphs over violence is more than just a dream; it urges us to work toward a society in which problems are handled through discussion and mutual respect.

Chapter 15: Looking Forward

The ongoing conflicts in the Middle East, particularly between Palestine and Israel, continue to cause severe disruption, with fighting consuming resources and claiming lives. This current upheaval is due to the long-running territorial conflicts in this region. The Yom Kippur War of 1973 shows an important historical parallel—lessons from which are still applicable today.

Between 6 and 25 October 1973, Israel stood alone against the Arab coalition led by Egypt and Syria in the War of Yom Kippur. It was a territorial struggle for land and dominance. In this surprise invasion, Egypt and Syria strove to recover the territory lost to Israel in the Six-Day War of 1967 at a huge cost in lives and material for both camps. Success for the invading forces in the early stages of the war was almost solely due to their ability to capitalize on the failures of Israeli intelligence, pointing out the sobering fact that, during wartime, preparation and competent intelligence are quite necessary.

External powers had an important influence on the Yom Kippur War and the present Middle Eastern crises. During the 1973 war, the United States and the Soviet Union offered major military and diplomatic assistance to their respective allies, Israel and the Arab states, impacting the conflict's results. Similarly, today's war has seen significant international involvement, with numerous nations contributing aid, military support, or diplomatic support to either Israel or Palestine. These additions further complicate the issue.

Both the Yom Kippur War and the ongoing wars have put an enormous burden on the global economy. The 1973 war prompted an oil embargo by Arab oil-producing countries, resulting in a worldwide energy crisis and emphasizing the extensive economic consequences of Middle Eastern conflicts. Continuous violence now interrupts economic activity, ruins infrastructure, and diverts national resources from development and welfare to military expenditure.

Diplomatically, the aftermath of the Yom Kippur War spurred substantial attempts toward peace and negotiation, most notably the Camp David Accords between Egypt and Israel, which resulted in a peace treaty and the restoration of the Sinai Peninsula to Egypt. These initiatives proved that negotiated agreements are feasible even after a violent confrontation. In the contemporary setting, pursuing peace remains a difficult but necessary objective, with numerous international initiatives aimed at mediating and resolving continuing conflicts.

The connections between the Yom Kippur War and today's crises emphasize the recurring themes of territorial disputes, international engagement, and the devastating human and economic costs of Middle Eastern combat. As the area continues to battle with complex and deeply ingrained difficulties, the lessons from the Yom Kippur War provide vital insights into the value of information, readiness, diplomacy, and the role of foreign powers in affecting war outcomes.

The 1973 Yom Kippur War taught us valuable lessons for modern military and political strategy in the Middle East and beyond. These lessons emphasize the value of information, readiness, foreign power engagement, psychological consequences, economic concerns, and diplomatic endeavors.

Israel's first failures during the Yom Kippur War were primarily the result of failing to foresee Egypt and Syria's coordinated strikes. This highlighted the importance of robust intelligence and military preparedness. Real-time information, surveillance, and reconnaissance (ISR) are critical components of modern military strategy for avoiding surprise assaults and ensuring fast reaction capabilities. Modern military spends heavily on technical breakthroughs such as drones, satellite imagery, and cyber intelligence to preserve a competitive advantage over possible enemies. The emphasis on enhanced ISR capabilities stems directly from the intelligence failures of the Yom Kippur War.

The psychological impact witnessed during the Yom Kippur War drove the development of psychological operations (PSYOPS) to become an important aspect of current military plans. The war damaged Israel's belief in invulnerability, emphasizing the significance of maintaining the morale and resilience of both military and civilian populations. Today, the military uses PSYOPS to affect enemies' perceptions and conduct. Building resilience through civil defense and public communication is critical for preserving national morale throughout long-term wars.

The 1973 oil embargo, which had sweeping implications, highlighted the economic elements of combat as well. Contemporary military plans must include potential economic consequences such as sanctions, trade disruptions, and resource scarcity. Military actions are frequently followed by economic measures aimed at reducing the adversary's ability to maintain combat. Furthermore, guaranteeing allied states' economic stability and post-conflict rehabilitation is vital for long-term peace and prosperity.

The Yom Kippur War stressed the need for military flexibility and innovation. Modern military plans emphasize adaptability and the capacity to respond swiftly to changing combat situations. This involves adopting new technology like artificial intelligence, cyber warfare capabilities, and enhanced defensive systems. Military training is increasingly geared at preparing soldiers for various circumstances, including asymmetric warfare and hybrid threats. The emphasis on technology superiority and adaptable methods directly relates to the technological and tactical obstacles encountered during the Yom Kippur War.

The notion of precision warfare, which originated in the Yom Kippur War, is now an essential component of modern military strategy. PGMs let troops hit hostile assets with high accuracy, resulting in little or no harm to friendly forces and innocent bystanders while drastically increasing operational effectiveness. This capacity has been substantially strengthened by network-centric warfare, which integrates platforms and sensors into a network for real-time data exchange and coordinated reactions, resulting in increased battlefield coordination and efficiency.

The extension of military operations into the space and cyber areas is an essential development in modern warfare. Satellites in space provide the safe transmission of crucial communications, navigation, and reconnaissance. Ensuring the security and resilience of those assets is critical to operational dominance. Cybersecurity is critical; governments are building complicated cyber-attack defenses as well as offensive cyber weapons that have the potential to destroy adversary networks and infrastructure.

The lessons from the Yom Kippur War have resulted in separate advancements in military strategy and development. Modern militaries utilize modern intelligence technologies and flexible training to increase their soldiers' skills in order to gain a strategic edge. Furthermore, further enhancements to the use of space and cyber domains broaden the scope of military operations, preparing for present and future wars. Armed forces are better able to handle the complexities of contemporary warfare and respond to emerging threats in a more interconnected world thanks to ongoing innovation and adaptability to new challenges.

The lessons from the Yom Kippur War have resulted in separate advancements in military strategy and development. Modern militaries deploy modern information systems, cutting-edge technology, psychological operations, economic measures, and adaptable training to increase their soldiers' skills and gain a strategic advantage. Furthermore, further enhancements to the use of space and cyber domains broaden the scope of military operations, preparing for present and future wars. Armed forces are better able to handle the complexities of contemporary warfare and respond to emerging threats in a more interconnected world thanks to ongoing innovation and adaptability to new challenges.

Strategically, it is seen as an important ally in the unstable area. To be more precise, during the Cold War, it served as a tool for fighting Soviet influence in the Middle East; now, it continues to function as a strategic ally in the fight against terrorism and ensuring regional security. The military and intelligence collaboration between the United States and Israel has significant mutual benefits. It serves as a forward post in the Middle East, providing valuable intelligence and regional influence to the United States.

The linkages in the commercial and technological sectors are very significant. Israel is one of the greatest purchasers of American military equipment and technology. This, in turn, supports the US defense sector and ensures that Israel maintains a qualitative military advantage over potential adversaries. Furthermore, it is a technological and innovation leader in Israel, particularly in cybersecurity, medical technology, and agriculture. Knowledge and technology exchange promotes economic and technical progress in both countries.

American support for Israel is also bound together by political and cultural ties. Different pro-Israel lobbying organizations, particularly AIPAC, exert a powerful influence in the U.S. political process in advancing policies aimed at strengthening relations between the United States and Israel. In addition to them being democracies with a view to civil liberties and respect for human rights, there is also a feeling of shared values and principles that unite the two. In addition, many Americans share Judeo-Christian values, creating an even closer cultural and religious relationship.

Humanitarian and ethical considerations underpin U.S. support as well. Having gone through several wars with neighbors and living with continuous security threats, the commitment of the United States to Israel's security is rightly regarded as a humanitarian imperative for safeguarding a democratic state and its citizens from threats to existence. It is a large financial aid, as the U.S. is providing substantial economic and military assistance to Israel so that it can defend itself without problems. It is part of larger foreign assistance programs to support stability and democracy in areas of interest.

Aside from the well-known causes, several other factors strengthen the tie between America and Israel. One of them is unquestionably the geopolitical reality of the Middle East, in which Israel manages to operate as a balancing force in an otherwise volatile region. The United States is consequently interested in stability, which includes the free flow of oil and restrictions against extreme organizations. Supporting Israel provides the United States with a reliable ally in the area, counterbalancing hostile governments and non-state entities.

Furthermore, the United States and Israel have extensive intelligence collaboration, which has greatly aided counterterrorism efforts. In truth, Israeli intelligence agencies may provide vital information that benefits US national security. This also extends to cybersecurity, as Israel's sophisticated technology helps to secure both nations against cyber-attacks.

Israel receives tremendous support from the American populace. Based on cultural, religious, and historical contexts, the vast majority of Americans hold a highly positive view of Israel. This has resonated in politics, as politicians and those providing services tend to reflect popular opinion by voting in support of good connections between the United States and Israel.

The notion that "Israel must not be allowed to lose" is based on historical, geographical, moral, and strategic concerns that emphasize the necessity of ensuring the State of Israel's security and survival. However, it is primarily founded on several fundamental assumptions, as well as the distinctiveness of Israel's position in the Middle East and across the world.

Historically, 1948 was the year Israel was created. It was a huge step toward giving a homeland for Jews after centuries of persecution by humanity, culminating in the Holocaust. The establishment of Israel not only fulfilled the Zionist goal, but it also addressed the critical need for a safe refuge for Jews worldwide. Within this historical context, the notion that Israel cannot afford to lose is intrinsically linked to the moral obligation to defend a nation founded from a terrible human tragedy and the right of countries to self-determination.

Israel is located in the Middle East, an area known for its continual instability, battles, and power struggles. The loss of Israel in some significant military or existential sense will most likely result in a power vacuum, which might have severe consequences for regional and global stability. Indeed, the state of Israel serves as a barrier against the spread of extreme ideas and hostile governments. Its military capabilities and intelligence services are crucial for combating terrorism and preventing the spread of weapons of mass destruction. As a result, it is assumed that Israel's security concerns must be addressed to maintain a status-quo balance of power, so deterring wider outbreaks of violence.

Furthermore, this notion's moral and ethical implications should not be neglected. The international community bears a duty to ensure that no nation, particularly one with Israel's history, confronts the prospect of destruction. Israel's right to exist and defend itself is a concept inscribed in international law and upheld by various United Nations resolutions. Allowing Israel to lose would not only contravene these values but would also establish a dangerous precedent, eroding international standards designed to defend sovereign states from existential dangers.

Israel's internal stability and wealth also serve as a shining example of democracy and innovation in a region where such principles are frequently threatened. Israel's accomplishments in technology, health, agriculture, and other disciplines have had a significant worldwide influence, highlighting the good contributions that may come from a strong and safe country. Ensuring Israel's survival also means keeping a paradigm of prosperity and advancement that may inspire and benefit the rest of the globe.

Chapter 16: 50 Years On – Echoes of Conflict

It all began with a rush of emotions: excitement, worry, and an overpowering sense of pride. Who could miss the rush of excitement for the many experiences ahead as we boarded that gigantic yacht that would become my home? Those early days were difficult, with extensive instruction, constant drilling, and a high learning curve. Its grandeur was daunting and terrifying, a continual reminder of my smallness in the broader scheme of things.

One of the most fundamental yet long-lasting things I've learned is the benefit of companionship. What actually linked shipmates to me so fast was that, in the face of arduous missions, terrible weather, and lengthy deployments away from home, the crew became my surrogate family. We celebrated wins together and helped each other through difficult times. There was an unwritten agreement that we had each other's backs, which provided strength and resiliency.

Life onboard was quite unpredictable. From pedaling through storms to unexpected order changes, I learned to adjust quickly. Flexibility became second nature, and as each new obstacle presented itself, I improved my ability to think on my feet. This was a critical adaptation for survival and personal development. I learned to accept unpredictability and be cool under pressure.

As I progressed through the ranks, additional duties arose. Leading a team necessitated more than just technical abilities; it also required empathy, patience, and motivation. Effective leadership entailed servicing people under my charge and cultivating an atmosphere based on trust and mutual respect. This leadership development extends beyond naval life to encounters and relationships on land.

Discipline was the foundation of life in the Navy. Everything had to be done in accordance with established regulations and protocols, from maintaining the ship's cleanliness to personal conduct. And, while I've realized that it instills order and efficiency, it also fosters character in its own way. It instilled in me a sense of pride in my profession as well as a great respect for the naval hierarchy and traditions.

She was a terrible mistress, the water. I suffered breakdowns and near-death experiences and was constantly pushed to my physical and emotional limits. Still, each hurdle I overcame made me a bit stronger. I realized that true strength isn't the absence of fear; it's the ability to carry on notwithstanding.

Long hours at sea provided enough opportunity for thought. I frequently think about the decisions I've made in my life, what is important to me, and what lies ahead. This personal reflection helped me grow as a person. I learned that it is critical to stand up for what I believe in and to never give up on a cause I believe in, no matter how difficult the circumstances.

Returning home was bittersweet. Despite missing critical occasions and turning points in my life, I got experiences and teachings that were worth more than gold. I went home with a renewed respect for family, freedom, and life's basic joys. The voyage taught me to cherish memories with appreciation and humility.

Brotherhood, flexibility, leadership, discipline, resilience, introspection, and thankfulness were the recurring themes that rang true during my time at sea. This was much more than a job; it was a life experience that supported and shaped me into a strong, honest, and smart individual.

The Yom Kippur War, also known as the October War, began in October 1973 and has significant lessons and ramifications for the present day. The war was a surprise attack by a coalition of Arab governments, namely Egypt and Syria, against Israel on Yom Kippur, the holiest day of Judaism. The conflict resulted in significant losses, with far-reaching political, military, and psychological consequences for the participating countries and beyond.

That is why understanding the Yom Kippur War is important. It reveals the complexity of geopolitics in the Middle East. There was a time in this war when the region was so volatile that deeply seated tension between Israel and its neighbors reflected a wide and broad connection to world politics. In understanding how this conflict took place, one can see the historical underpinnings of continuing disputes and the intricate, continuing dynamics that shape the region today.

This war also brought with it the rudest reminder of the price that comes with being unprepared and just how important intelligence is to any nation's security. Israel won in the end through its military power, but at the same time was caught off guard by the attack. So much so that it was seriously reconsidering its position regarding intelligence and defense strategies, henceforth informing us of its approach toward security. From this example, modern nations can draw a lesson in the value of being vigilant at all times and integrating intelligence into national defense planning appropriately.

One of the abiding lessons from the Yom Kippur War is the importance of diplomacy in conflict resolution. Eventually, the battle resulted in the Camp David Agreements of 1978, one of the major peace deals between Egypt and Israel, with the United States serving as broker. This peace deal not only altered West Asia's political dynamics but also demonstrated that even the most entrenched disputes can be resolved via discussion and diplomacy. Today, this is an extremely relevant lesson to contemplate as the globe continues to grapple with countless conflicts and seeks paths to peace.

The economic impact of the Yom Kippur War has important implications for modern world economies. The war prompted an oil embargo by Arab oil producers, pushed the globe into an energy crisis, and demonstrated how, with interconnected economies, regional wars may have far-reaching consequences throughout the world. Understanding these processes is critical in today's world, when economies are becoming increasingly interconnected. This, in turn, serves as a cautionary narrative about the possible global economic consequences of regional instability.

The human cost of the Yom Kippur War emphasizes the widespread devastation that armed conflict generates. Some of the unpleasant lessons gained regarding the human cost of war include murdering individuals, relocating populations, and psychological disorders among those engaged. This prioritizes conflict avoidance, humanitarian relief, and post-conflict reconstruction to alleviate suffering among impacted communities.

The 1973 Yom Kippur War demonstrates the resilience and adaptation that nations and peoples may possess. Following initial defeats, the Israeli force was able to reorganize, changing the direction of the conflict. This demonstrates the power and endurance with which the human spirit can overcome adversity—a lesson applicable when nations face other crises, such as a pandemic or another type of calamity.

Since 1948, there have been far too many conflicts. The human and financial costs of these conflicts have been too high. Approximately 23 million individuals have died in wars, including military troops and civilians. It varies widely depending on the geography and the intensity of the battle, but the human toll is significant. Specifically, the conflicts that followed the 9/11 attacks in Iraq, Afghanistan, Syria, Yemen, and Pakistan killed at least 940,000 people directly connected to war, including around 432,000 civilians.

If one adds up the financial expenditure on wars since the year 1948, it reaches a huge amount. The United States alone has spent more than $5.9 trillion for wars in Iraq, Syria, Afghanistan, and Pakistan, among others, since the year 2001. This includes direct military expenditure, veteran care, and interest on funds borrowed to carry out these wars. In the Middle East, the conflicts cost around $11 trillion since 1948 and dealt a severe blow to the economies of Iraq, Syria, and Yemen.

These conflicts have not only depleted massive financial resources but have also resulted in major humanitarian disasters, displacing millions. For example, since the commencement of the post-9/11 hostilities, a minimum of 38 million people have been displaced inside and across nations. Economic consequences extend beyond immediate military expenditure to global economies, and humanitarian help and rehabilitation initiatives need long-term support. These figures provide a more detailed knowledge of how wars harm mankind and global security, emphasizing the importance of establishing diplomatic solutions and conflict prevention efforts to avoid such disastrous repercussions in the future.

Beyond the enormous figures of lives lost and money spent, the impacts of these conflicts are felt throughout generations. It is typically followed by long-term economic instability in the impacted areas. Countries that have been the target of prolonged wars must face the immediate expenses of war and the difficulty of rebuilding their economies and infrastructure. Such areas see disruptions in economic activity, the destruction of critical infrastructure, and a large loss of human capital, all of which limit development and prolong cycles of poverty and insecurity.

Furthermore, such wars have a devastating environmental impact. Pollution and land degradation are common in war zones and can have long-term consequences for ecosystems and humans. Environmental deterioration will further complicate recovery efforts and reduce agricultural production, resulting in food insecurity in already vulnerable communities.

These broad repercussions underline the crucial need to seek diplomatic solutions and preventive steps to resolve conflicts, underlining the need for international collaboration and a holistic approach to peacebuilding. Understanding these consequences emphasizes the need to learn from history and work toward a more peaceful and stable world.

Certain approaches can be incorporated when dealing with international affairs that can significantly reduce the loss of life and damage of land that occurs after every war;

Diplomacy is used to find a solution that avoids conflict. Communication, negotiation, and peace talks are all methods for resolving conflicts and finding common ground among the people concerned. International institutions such as the United Nations provide the globe with a venue for resolving problems and developing peaceful solutions. The Camp David peace pact between Egypt and Israel is only one of several peace treaties that have been negotiated by stringent diplomatic efforts, demonstrating the strength of such processes.

Economic instability and poverty are frequently the root causes of violence. Investing in economic growth, generating employment opportunities, and reducing poverty may all contribute to regional stability and conflict prevention. Programs that promote sustainable development and equitable resource distribution can alleviate the socioeconomic gaps that frequently contribute to violence. Improving international institutions and systems that promote peace and security is critical. Organizations such as the United Nations, the International Criminal Court, and regional groups can be strengthened to better avoid conflicts and respond to them when they occur. These institutions can adopt collaboration and provide venues for conflict resolution.

The promotion of education and the creation of awareness about the dangers of war and the advantages brought about by peace is critical. Education may foster a culture of peace, tolerance, and mutual respect. It may also offer people the ability and knowledge to settle problems nonviolently. Peace education programs in schools and communities have the potential for long-term reduction of violence. Implementing early warning systems to predict possible conflicts allows for prompt actions. Governments and international organizations can prevent conflicts from escalating by monitoring political, social, and economic factors. This includes collecting intelligence, evaluating data, and coordinating responses to new threats.

The potential for weapons to harm cannot be reduced without at least some limitation on their availability. International treaties, such as the Treaty on the Non-Proliferation of Nuclear Weapons and the Armaments Trade Treaty, include mechanisms for regulating armament circulation and encouraging disarmament. Halting illegal arms transactions and reducing the stockpile of weapons also calls for effort. Lowering the harmful potential of weapons through limitation of availability will eventually ensure world safety and peace.

Prioritizing humanity is arguably the only possible way to avoid war. This means considering the value of human life in all choices and actions. Encouraging understanding and cooperation between people and nations addresses the root causes of conflict. Encouraging conversation and peaceful agreements over violent clashes leads to long-term outcomes. When humanity is valued, choices are made with people's well-being in mind, lowering the risk of conflict and creating a more peaceful society.

I may have been heavily involved in the navy, and my role was one that emphasized the protection of my nation, but after witnessing the bloodshed firsthand, I would urge those in power to choose peace over conflict and violence, that's all.

Afterword

On December 1, 1973, the crew of the USS John F. Kennedy felt a feeling of relief when it moored at Mayport, Florida. The Yom Kippur War had taxed their resolve, but they were now back home. Steve, Philip, and I stood together, feeling the weight of the previous month lift as we rejoined with our families. The war had taken its toll, yet our friendship was stronger than ever.

Reflecting on the Yom Kippur War, I understood that the feeling of responsibility and sacrifices made along the road had transformed me. Our aim was clear: to help Israel in its moment of need. Operation Nickel Grass, the United States airlift that delivered critical supplies to Israel, was a watershed moment. I was truly gratified that our efforts had contributed to assuring Israel's existence.

The battle also revealed the fragility of peace. I saw the damage wrought by conflict and the careful balance required to avert future escalation. Henry Kissinger's shuttle diplomacy, which included negotiating ceasefires and controlling superpower participation, was a lesson in strategic negotiation. This event increased my understanding of the complexities of international politics and the value of faithful allies.

Returning home was bittersweet. There was delight in reconciling with loved ones, but we veterans also had a common awareness of what we had gone through. The Yom Kippur War changed the geopolitical environment and had a long-term influence on those of us who served.

Steve, Philip, and I frequently pondered about our time at sea, particularly the moments of amity that had gotten us through the most difficult days. We knew our experiences had formed a friendship that would endure a lifetime. Our service demonstrated our resilience and dedication to a higher purpose.

The Yom Kippur War taught me the importance of responsibility and the resilience of the human spirit.

I remembered the men and women who gave their lives for freedom and justice during idle hours. Their selflessness reminds us of the high cost of conflict and the possibility of peace. I hung on to this hope, hoping that understanding, conversation, and a dedication to humanity may lead to a more peaceful future.

Ralph Waldo Emerson famously stated, "The real and lasting victories are those of peace, not war."

As I faced my future, I vowed to honor this reality by carrying on the legacy of those who had served beside me in the search for a better world.

Printed in the USA
CPSIA information can be obtained
at www.ICGtesting.com
CBHW051801180824
13303CB00039B/893

9 798895 257517